COOKING
with
CHICKEN

Marshall Cavendish

Picture Credits

Alan Duns: 1, 4/5, 8/9, 11, 94, 95, 96

Melvin Grey: 37, 39, 44/5, 46/7, 48/9, 50/1, 52/3, 54/5, 57, 86/7

Gina Harris: 26, 28/9, 34/5, 36

Anthony Kay: 58/9, 61, 63, 64/5

John Lee: 77, 84/5

David Levin: 3, 6/7, 15, 16/17, 19, 20/1, 30/31, 32/3, 40/1, 42, 43, 79, 80, 81, 90, 91, 92, 93

Moulinex Ltd: 13

Roger Phillips: 69, 71, 72, 74, 76, 83

Iain Reid: 14, 22/3, 24

Swiss Turkey: 30/31, 32/3

Paul Williams: 67/8, 70

George Wright: 12, 88/9

Published by
Marshall Cavendish Books Limited
58 Old Compton Street
London W1V 5PA

© Marshall Cavendish Limited 1976-84

This volume first published 1979

ISBN 0 85685 154 X

Printed and bound in Italy by New Interlitho SpA.

CONTENTS

Finger lickin' chicken

Now that chicken is always available, pennywise cooks are constantly on the look out for new ways of cooking it. Grilling is often thought to be a rather dull way to cook chicken but if tangy herbs and spicy sauces are added it becomes deliciously interesting. Here you are shown how to choose for flavour, divide into portions and grill to perfection.

Thanks to agricultural progress chicken, once a luxury food reserved for high days and holidays, is now cheap enough to eat for everyday meals. There are sceptics who say that today's intensively reared birds taste just like cardboard but, cooked with flair, modern chickens are just as good and tasty as those of days gone by.

With suitable young birds, grilling is the simplest and most variable method of cooking. It enhances the flavour, retains the natural succulence of the bird and results in crisp, golden brown skin. Fresh birds can be grilled simply with herbs or a delicate basting sauce, while frozen birds can be given extra flavour with a robust sauce or topping.

Here we show how to divide both large and small birds. Small, young

The marinade used for Devilled chicken Delmonico is thickened with breadcrumbs and spooned over chicken before final cooking

birds are best for grilling. If serving, say, 8 people, it is better to buy two small birds and to cut each into 4 portions rather than to cut one large bird into 8 pieces.

CHOOSING CHICKEN

Chickens for cooking by methods other than boiling or long casseroling are all specially reared so that they will put on the maximum of tender flesh at minimum cost to the producer. Almost all chickens sold in poulterers, butchers and markets are reared indoors under controlled conditions. Outdoor or free-range chickens are rarely seen these days, partly because they are uneconomic, but mainly because their quality is difficult to control and it is hard to guarantee that the customer will always get a tender, tasty bird. It is in fact something of a myth that these free-range birds taste better. Because outdoor chickens run around and eat at will, they are prone to disease and liable to develop rather more muscle and sinew than is desirable for a tender grilling or roasting bird.

It is the processing method after killing, not the rearing, that most affects the quality of the chicken you buy and, for this reason, it is important to go to a butcher or poulterer if you want a really well-flavoured bird. There are several types and sizes of chicken available. These are described in the chart. Chickens are processed in four different ways: fresh, farm fresh, chilled and frozen.

Fresh chickens

Fresh chickens are seen in butchers' and poulterers' shops either feathered or plucked out with head and feet left on (known as New York dressed). These chickens come to the butcher with their feathers on. He then hangs them for about three days

Types of chicken suitable for grilling

Type	Description	Method
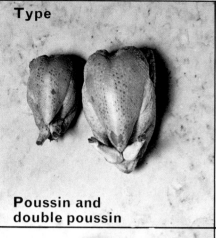 **Poussin and double poussin**	Both available fresh, farm fresh, chilled or frozen. Poussins are killed when 4 weeks old and usually weigh about 450 g [1 lb], which means they will only serve 1 portion as the ratio of bone to meat is rather high. Double poussins are killed when about 6 weeks old and weigh about 1 kg [2 lb]. They can be cut in half or spatch-cocked to serve 2 portions. One double poussin between two is better value than a whole poussin each.	The most satisfactory way of cooking poussins is en cocotte or by pot roasting, although it is possible to spatchcock them, that is, opened out flat and skewered for grilling. Season, brush with butter or oil and grill for 10 minutes, skin side down, 12 cm [5"] away from medium heat. Turn and grill for another 8 minutes, basting occasionally. Double poussins are grilled as for a poussin but increase grilling time by 2-3 minutes on each side, depending on size.
 **Spring chicken**	Available fresh, farm fresh, chilled and sometimes frozen. Spring chickens are not reared in the spring as the name might suggest but are killed when 8 weeks old. They have an average weight of 1¼-1½ kg [2½-3 lb] and may be roasted or divided into portions for grilling.	Grill as for poussins, increasing the grilling time by 2-3 minutes each side, depending on the thickness of the pieces. Add the thinner breast portions to the grill 5 minutes after starting to cook the leg portions.
Roaster	Sometimes also called a broiler (not to be confused with a boiler which is a much older bird), these chickens are available fresh, farm fresh, chilled, frozen or cut into portions. A roasting chicken is killed when it is between 8 and 10 weeks old and usually weighs from 1½-3 kg [3-6 lb], and is suitable for roasting whole or grilling divided into portions.	Season, brush with butter or oil and grill for 12 minutes, skin side down, 12 cm [5"] away from medium heat. Turn and grill for a further 10 minutes, basting occasionally. Increase grill-ing time for very thick pieces and add thinner breast pieces 5 minutes after the legs.
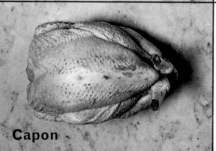 **Capon**	Available fresh, farm fresh, chilled and sometimes frozen, capons are male birds which have been treated with female hormones to make them put on a lot of weight in a short time. Capons are usually killed when 8 weeks old and weigh from 3-4 kg [6-8 lb]. Capons are suitable for roasting whole or dividing into portions and grilling.	Grill as for roaster portions. Cook as above, depending on size.

to allow the maximum flavour to develop before preparing for selling.

Look for chickens with smooth, unbroken flesh, a slightly pliable beak and breastbone and pale yellow legs with small scales. All these factors indicate a young, tender bird.

If you buy a New York dressed or feathered chicken, the butcher will charge you for the total weight of the bird before he has removed the head, feet, feathers and innards (called drawing or eviscerating). These

'extras' can add up to 1 kg [2 lb] to the weight of the bird, depending on its size, so always take this into account when buying. If you are unsure of how much to buy, ask the butcher. Make sure you take the giblets and feet with you to use for stock or giblet gravy.

Because selling chickens in this way is a fairly labour-intensive pro-cess they tend to be expensive but hanging does mean that the flavour is good.

Farm-fresh chickens
Farm-fresh chickens are hung and prepared for selling on the poultry farm. They are usually sold whole, oven ready with the giblets in a little bag inside. Once again, this is a labour-intensive process so the chickens cost more but taste good. You are not, however, paying for unusable parts as when buying a New York dressed chicken as the head, feet and innards have been removed before selling.

Chilled chickens

Chilled chickens are usually seen in chain stores. They are factory-produced birds, reared by intensive methods, killed when a certain weight (usually 1.4-1.7 kg [3-3½ lb]) is reached, plucked, eviscerated, then air-chilled immediately without hanging. Air-chilling is a dry method so the bird does not take in water as with a frozen chicken. For this reason, chilled chickens are slightly more expensive than frozen chickens. Chilled chickens are available oven ready, halved or as portions. They are always marked as chilled on the wrapping.

Frozen chickens

Frozen chickens are reared and killed in exactly the same way as chilled chickens and are usually sold in supermarkets and chain stores. The only difference is that in the freezing process the bird takes in quite a lot of water. The chicken is weighed after freezing and, in some cases, you may be paying for rather a high ratio of water to flesh. It also has a slight effect on flavour though expert opinion says that, if thawed correctly, frozen chicken is as good in flavour as chilled. Frozen chicken is available oven ready with the giblets in a little bag (usually placed in the cavity), halved or divided into portions.

How much to buy

Knowing how much to buy is always a problem with birds as their odd shape makes it hard to judge. Below is a quantity guideline for serving chicken plainly grilled. If the recipe you are using has several garnishes or a sauce, this amount can be decreased. All weights are for oven-ready birds (plucked and drawn, with head and feet removed) so, if buying fresh chicken, ask the butcher for a bird of whatever weight you require after drawing.

For two people you will need two poussins weighing 450 g [1 lb] each or one 700 g-1 kg [1½-2 lb] double poussin or spring chicken cut in half.

For four people choose a 1¼-1½ kg [2½-3½ lb] broiler and cut it into portions as shown in the step-by-step instructions.

For six people choose a 2.75-3.6 kg [6-8 lb] capon and cut it into joints as shown in the step-by-step instructions.

When serving chicken joints allow 1 large quarter or 1 breast or 2 drumsticks or 2 thighs per person. Wings are not really substantial enough to serve unless they are cut with a large portion of the breast attached, as shown in quartering chicken step-by-step.

STORING

Chicken, like all meat, is perishable and must be stored carefully to preserve goodness.

Fresh and farm-fresh chickens and portions

Remove butcher's wrapping and put the chicken on a plate. If the giblets are in a bag inside the bird, remove them. Cover the chicken lightly with greaseproof paper or kitchen foil to allow a little circulation of air and store in the coldest part of the refrigerator under the frozen food compartment. Whole birds will keep for 2-3 days, portions for a maximum of 36 hours. Alternatively, you can store whole birds in a cool larder for 1 day but never do this in warm weather as the flavour will go 'off' very quickly.

Chilled birds

Store the chicken in the polythene wrapping in which you bought it but loosen the wrapping a little to allow circulation of air and remove the giblets. Store in a refrigerator or larder, as for fresh or farm-fresh chickens.

Frozen birds

These must be placed in the freezer or the freezer compartment of a refrigerator as soon as you get them home. Store for up to 3 months, depending on the star rating of your refrigerator.

Cooked chicken

Cooked chicken joints are excellent picnic and packed lunch fare, but go 'off' very quickly so they must always be stored in a refrigerator and should be eaten within two days. If you plan to eat chicken cold, drain off any liquid immediately after cooking then cool the meat rapidly. As soon as the chicken is cold, wrap it loosely (in polythene, kitchen foil or shrink wrapping) to protect against drying out, to prevent infection and the transfer of food flavours. Refrigerate.

PREPARING

If you are planning to serve chicken joints, it is much cheaper to buy a whole bird and divide it up yourself. Although this might sound a daunting prospect, it is really very easy.

Equipment

To portion a chicken you will need a really sharp, large cook's knife. A good sharp knife will cut easily through bones and flesh. A blunt or serrated-edge knife should be avoided as it will tear the flesh.

If you find a knife awkward it may well be worth investing in a pair of poultry shears. These are large scissor-like implements with strong curved blades. A useful alternative to poultry shears, and especially good for cutting through chicken backbones, is a strong pair of kitchen scissors. The kind which are nicked at the bottom of the blades are best because they make cutting up poultry easier.

You will need a chopping board on which to stand the chicken.

Thawing

Before a frozen chicken can be cut into pieces, it must be thawed. For health reasons, it is most important to thaw chicken very thoroughly. Chickens contain tiny bacilli called salmonella. These are quite harmless when the chicken is cooked right through. If the chicken is not thawed

fully there will be a cold spot at the centre which will not cook quite as well as the rest of the bird. The bacilli remain active in this undercooked portion and, if eaten, can cause an attack of a particularly unpleasant and virulent form of food poisoning.

Frozen whole birds and portions sometimes come with thawing instructions and these should always be followed meticulously. When thawing chicken, leave it in the wrapping to avoid loss of juices.

The best place to thaw is in the refrigerator. When thawing a whole bird in the refrigerator, allow 5 hours per 450 g [1 lb] of chicken. This means a 1.4 kg [3 lb] chicken needs 15 hours to thaw properly. Portions will take about 6 hours. Chicken can be thawed at room temperature but this is a quicker process and is not quite so kind to the flavour of the bird as gradual thawing. When thawing at room temperature, allow 3 hours per 450 g [1 lb] of whole bird. Portions will need about 3 hours.

In an emergency, chicken thawing can be hastened by immersing the bird (still in its polythene wrapping) in cold water. This makes the flavour extremely bland and is not really advisable. Never immerse chicken in hot water to speed thawing. It makes the flesh tough and does not thaw thoroughly.

Preparing for jointing
Before you start cutting up your chicken, make sure the giblets have been removed from inside.

To make cutting easier, it is a good idea to cut off the loose flap of skin at the neck end. Scissors are best for this job as the skin is rather awkward to cut with a knife.

You may also wish to remove the little oil sac situated above the parson's nose (the pointed end of the chicken where its tail feathers used to be). This little sac contains a rather strong oil which the chicken uses to lubricate its feathers. Some people feel it gives a fishy flavour. Removing the parson's nose itself is the subject of controversy. Some families have battles over who gets the parson's nose, while others regard it with horror, so this is very much a matter of personal taste.

There may be some little bits of feather left over after plucking. These are usually found on the legs and wings and are quite easily removed by pulling gently.

Removing the bony tips of the wings depends very much on what you are going to do with the chicken. If you are cutting large wing portions with a piece of breast attached, it is a good idea to leave the wing tips on as they help to make a neat shape. Leave the tips on, too, if trussing a whole bird for spit roasting or grilling. The wing tips can always be cut off after cooking. Cutting off after cooking is quick to do as the bones become very soft.

On a fresh chicken, there may be a piece of yellow leg left on the end of the drumstick. Cut this off before starting preparation.

GRILLING CHICKEN
One of the joys of chicken is that, after cutting it into halves or portions, it needs very little else in the way of preparation before being grilled.

Advance preparation
Because chicken is a fairly dry meat, portions and halves must be brushed liberally inside and out with melted butter or olive oil before grilling. Cut surfaces of chicken are small and, unlike other meats, raw chicken does not bleed when salt is applied so seasoning can be done before cooking. This is in fact quite a good idea because salt crisps the skin.

Grilling
Because chicken is dry and delicately flavoured, grilling must be carried out under gentle heat throughout. This is achieved by positioning the grill pan 12-15 cm [5-6"] below the grill and setting the heat at about medium. There is no need to start grilling under fierce heat to seal the cut surfaces. This is because chicken is not red meat and, therefore, does not lose blood and juice as is the case in pork, lamb and beef. Also, cut surfaces with portions and halves are rather small.

Start grilling the chicken skin side down. Grill large portions and halves for 12-15 minutes, small portions for 8-12 minutes. Turn skin side up and grill large portions and halves for a further 10 minutes, small portions for 8 minutes. Baste with melted butter throughout cooking to prevent drying.

SPATCHCOCK CHICKEN
This is a very simple dish and, in order to ensure its success, be sure to use a fresh, plump double poussin.

Although it is usual to start grilling the chicken skin side down, here the order is reversed and the chicken is

Spatchcock chicken served with chips and garnished with lemon and watercress makes an appetizing main course.

Step-by-step to chicken portions

1 Lay the chicken on a board. Cut off the oil sac and the parson's nose if wished. Then cut off the loose skin at the neck.

2 To halve the chicken, cut through and along the breastbone. The breastbone is very soft, so a sharp knife will do this easily.

3 Then cut through the backbone. If the backbone is too hard to cut with a sharp knife, use poultry shears or kitchen scissors.

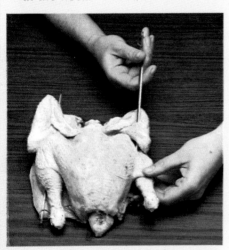

5 Now run a sharp, straight skewer through the leg and the fleshy part of the wing at one side. Repeat at other side.

6 To make chicken quarters, first cut the chicken in half. Lay the halves skin side up and cut diagonally between the leg and wing.

7 To joint a large chicken, first cut the leg away from the body. Pull the leg towards you so that the joint is exposed.

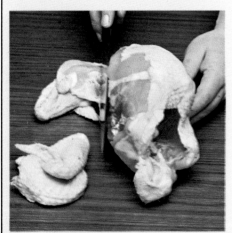

10 Cut through the joint to sever the wing and fold it into a neat shape with the attached breast meat tucked underneath.

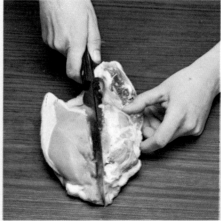

11 To remove the whole breast, first separate from the back by cutting through the rib bones along the side of the body.

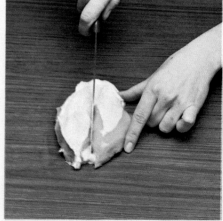

12 Cut down the centre of the breastbone to divide the breast into 2. Large breasts may be divided again to make 4 portions.

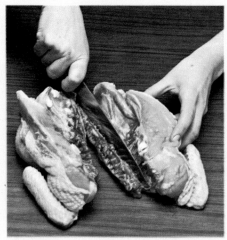

OR to remove the backbone completely, cut along each side of it with a sharp knife and then lift out. Save for stockmaking.

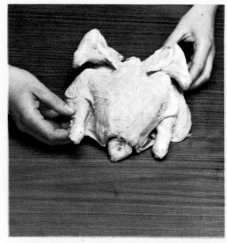

4 To spatchcock a chicken, first cut it in half through the backbone and open it out so that it lies flat on the board.

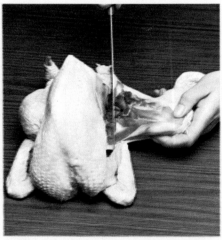

8 Now cut through the pink, moist part of this 'ball and socket' joint. Cut off the other leg. Set the two severed legs aside.

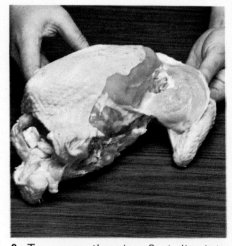

9 To remove the wing, first slice into the white breast meat to make a better portion. Pull the wings away to expose the joint.

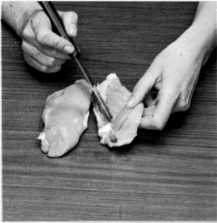

13 To skin the breast, pull away gently. To bone, insert a knife between rib bones and flesh and cut away gently. Save for stock.

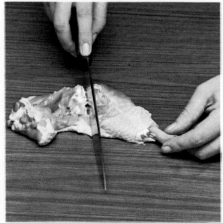

14 Large legs may be divided into thighs and drumsticks by cutting through the centre ball and socket joint.

grilled skin side up, turned skin side down and then, to finish, skin side up again. This last stage is to brown the breadcrumb mixture.

SERVES 2
1 double poussin, about 700 g [1½ lb] in weight
salt and pepper
half a lemon
50 g [2 oz] butter
25 g [1 oz] grated Parmesan cheese
1 thick slice two-day-old white bread

For the garnish:
2 lemon quarters
1 small packet straw potatoes
bunch of watercress

1 Cut off the leg shanks, parson's nose and loose neck skin.

2 Cut the chicken open right along the backbone.

3 Open the bird and press it flat.

4 Secure the bird by running a fine skewer through from the lower thigh to the wing on each side.

5 Rub the chicken with the cut lemon, season with salt and pepper and leave for 30 minutes in a cool place.

6 Heat the grill to medium. Melt the butter in a small pan.

7 Brush the chicken all over with melted butter.

8 Place the bird skin side up on the grid. Grill 12 cm [5"] below the heat for 8-10 minutes. Brush with more butter once during this time.

9 Turn the chicken over and grill the cut side for 10-12 minutes, basting it during this time.

10 Meanwhile, remove crust from bread and grate the bread on a grater over a plate (or use a liquidizer) to make 15 g [½ oz] fine crumbs.

11 Mix the breadcrumbs and the Parmesan cheese together.

12 Turn over the chicken again and sprinkle the skin evenly with the breadcrumb mixture.

Milanese chicken consists of boned chicken breasts topped with ham and tomatoes.

13 Dribble remaining melted butter from the saucepan (or spoon it from the grill pan base) over the crumbs, moistening them as evenly as possible.

14 Grill for a further 5-10 minutes until crisp and golden. Run a skewer into the thickest part of the chicken to see that juices run clear. If juices are clear the chicken is cooked. Pink juices indicate that further grilling is required.

15 Remove skewers and serve garnished with warm straw potatoes, wedges of lemon and watercress.

MILANESE CHICKEN

This is an excellent dish for a dinner party. Once the preliminary cooking is done the dish continues cooking in a very low oven until you are ready for it.

You can buy 2 chickens and cut the breasts off them (each chicken will give 2 portions) and save the rest of the meat for another dish. Alternatively, you can buy 4 portions of breast meat—the butcher will normally sell frozen portions.

SERVES 4
4 chicken breasts
4 slices ham
salt
2 medium-sized tomatoes
40 g [1½ oz] grated Parmesan cheese

For the marinade:
30 ml [2 tablespoons] oil
30 ml [2 tablespoons] lemon juice
5 ml [1 teaspoon] salt
freshly ground black pepper

1 Work a sharp knife along the bones to loosen and then pull the meat away by hand so that the breasts are boneless. Remove all the skin and any attached fat.

2 Lay the breasts flat, in a single layer and a small space apart, between 2 sheets of greaseproof paper. Beat hard with a rolling pin to flatten the meat.

3 Mix all the ingredients for the marinade and pour into a shallow,

flame-proof dish large enough to hold the chicken pieces flat in a single layer.

4 Put in the chicken breasts, turn in the marinade, cover the dish and leave in a cool place for 2 hours.

5 One hour before serving time, heat the grill. Heat the oven to 150°C [300°F] gas mark 2.

6 Uncover the chicken and put the flame-proof dish 12 cm [5"] below the grill. Grill each side 5 minutes.

7 Meanwhile, plunge the tomatoes into boiling water for 1 minute, drain and refresh under cold water, then peel away the skins. Cut each tomato into 4 slices.

8 Remove chicken from under grill. Arrange a slice of ham on top of each of the chicken breasts. Top each with 2 tomato slices. Sprinkle on half of the Parmesan cheese and then cover the dish with foil.

9 Transfer to the oven and leave for 30-40 minutes. (They won't spoil at this low temperature if left a little longer.)

10 Five minutes before serving, heat the grill. Remove the dish from the oven, take off the foil, sprinkle the tops of the tomatoes with remaining Parmesan cheese and brown quickly under the grill.

11 Serve immediately.

DEVILLED CHICKEN DELMONICO

Frozen chicken quarters can be used for this dish as the spicy devilled sauce will keep the joints moist and enhance the flavour. The chicken must be completely thawed before cooking, of course, so allow adequate time for this if using frozen chicken quarters. Cooking is finished in the oven so it is a useful dish when you are entertaining. Served cold, it makes a piquant picnic meal.

SERVES 4
1 kg [2½ lb] chicken or 4 chicken portions
3 slices of two-day-old bread

For the devil spread:
65 g [2½ oz] butter
5 ml [1 teaspoon] mustard powder
10 ml [2 teaspoons] curry powder
10 ml [2 teaspoons] caster sugar
2.5 ml [½ teaspoon] salt
2.5 ml [½ teaspoon] paprika
5 ml [1 teaspoon] Worcestershire sauce

1 If using a whole chicken, halve it by cutting along the breastbone. Open the chicken and cut along the backbone. Remove the backbone and cut the chicken into quarters.

2 Turn the wing tips under and run a fine skewer through the leg and backbone to hold the joints flat while cooking.

3 Prepare the devil spread by melting the butter in a small pan over low heat. Stir in the remaining ingredients.

4 Heat the grill to medium heat and warm the oven to 180°C [350°F] gas mark 4.

5 Brush the chicken pieces on both sides with half the devil mixture. Lay the pieces skin side down and side by side in a shallow flame-proof dish.

6 Place the chicken dish 12 cm [5"] below the heat and grill for 5 minutes on each side.

7 Meanwhile, remove crusts from the bread and reduce to crumbs on a grater or in a liquidizer to make 50 g [2 oz] fine crumbs.

8 Re-heat the devilled mixture remaining in the saucepan. Add the crumbs, remove from heat and stir until crumbs have absorbed the liquid.

9 Spoon the crumbs evenly over the chicken pieces and transfer the dish to the centre of the oven.

10 Cook for 30 minutes. Serve hot or cold.

CHICKEN IN SPICY TOMATO SAUCE

This is the type of dish that soon becomes a family favourite. It is colourful, tasty and simple—suited to fresh or frozen chicken joints.

SERVES 4
4 chicken portions
50 g [2 oz] butter

For the sauce:
60 ml [4 tablespoons] tomato ketchup
15 ml [1 tablespoon] finely grated onion
30 ml [2 tablespoons] water
30 ml [2 tablespoons] wine vinegar
10 ml [2 teaspoons] soft brown sugar
2.5 ml [½ teaspoon] mustard powder
2.5 ml [½ teaspoon] salt

For the garnish:
bunch of watercress

1 Heat the grill to medium heat.

2 Melt the butter in a small sauce-pan. Brush the chicken joints all over with butter.

3 Remove the grid from the grill pan and arrange the chicken pieces, skin side down and side by side, in the bottom of the grill pan, or in a large flame-proof gratin dish.

4 Grill the chicken 12 cm [5"] away from the heat for 5 minutes. Turn the chicken over and grill for another 5 minutes.

5 Meanwhile, grate the onion over a plate to catch the juice.

6 Put the onion into the saucepan containing the remaining melted butter. Stir in the other sauce ingredients and simmer for 5 minutes.

7 Brush the chicken with the sauce and continue grilling under moderate heat, turning and brushing with more sauce every 5 minutes until the chicken is cooked right through, a total of 30 minutes.

8 If the grill pan was used, turn the chicken pieces on to a hot serving dish and spoon the sauce on top. Garnish with watercress.

COUNTRY-STYLE CHICKEN
This is a simple but attractive way of cooking chicken. Fresh chicken is recommended. Use a whole chicken and divide it into portions yourself (it's probably cheaper too) but if you are in a hurry you can buy chicken joints. If you buy fresh chicken joints on your way home you can have this dish ready to eat within 45 minutes of arriving in the kitchen. The skewers are run through the chicken to prevent the joints 'flying akimbo' during grilling, in which case some parts would be cooked before others as they would be closer to the heat.

SERVES 4
1 kg [2½ lb] chicken
1 large lemon
75 g [3 oz] butter
salt
freshly ground black pepper
4 large rashers of streaky bacon
225 g [½ lb] button mushrooms

For the garnish:
bunch of watercress

1 Heat the grill to medium heat.

2 Divide the chicken into halves by cutting along the breastbone. Open the chicken and cut along the backbone. Cut the chicken into quarters.

3 Run a small skewer through each leg and out by the backbone. Tuck the wing tips under.

4 Rub the chicken with the cut lemon, squeezing the lemon to release plenty of juice as you do so.

5 Melt the butter in a small pan and brush generously all over both sides of the chicken.

6 Sprinkle both sides of the chicken liberally with salt and lightly with pepper.

7 Lay the joints skin side down in the grill pan with the grid removed.

8 Place the chicken 12 cm [5"] below the grill and cook for 12-15 minutes.

9 Meanwhile, de-rind the bacon and cut each rasher in half crossways. Roll up and secure each piece with a cocktail stick.

10 Remove earthy ends, wipe but do not peel the mushrooms and brush over with some of the butter.

11 Turn the chicken skin side up, brush with remaining melted butter, or baste with the grill pan juices, and continue grilling for 5 minutes.

12 Add the bacon rolls and mushrooms around the chicken under the grill. Baste with the pan juices.

13 Continue grilling and lower the heat if the chicken shows signs of overbrowning. Turn the bacon and mushrooms to cook them on both sides, basting them as you do so.

14 Cook until the chicken's skin is brown and crisp and the bacon and mushrooms are ready.

15 Arrange the cooked chicken on a serving dish. Arrange the bacon and mushrooms around it and pour over any remaining lemon juice and the juices from the grill pan. Garnish with the watercress and serve immediately.

Variations
● For almond chicken, omit the bacon and mushrooms and instead fry 40 g [1½ oz] flaked almonds in a little butter for 1 minute until golden brown. Do this just before serving the chicken. Use medium heat and shake the pan to turn the nuts frequently to prevent burning. Add the lemon juice and pour over the grilled chicken. Serve immediately.

● For pineapple chipolata, omit the bacon and mushrooms. Brush 4 pineapple rings with butter and grill until golden. Grill 4 chipolata sausages at the same time and thread them through the pineapple rings for the garnish. Arrange on top of the grilled chicken in the serving dish.

BROILED CHICKEN WITH LEMON BARBECUE SAUCE
Here is an American recipe which gives the chicken an unusual flavour. You need to start preparations a couple of hours ahead to give the chicken time to marinate in the sauce. Fresh chicken is best for this recipe but you could use frozen chicken because the marinade will add flavour. (Broiled is the American word for grilled.)

SERVES 4
4 chicken portions

For the marinade:
1 garlic clove
5 ml [1 teaspoon] salt
2.5 ml [½ teaspoon] freshly ground black pepper
45 ml [3 tablespoons] oil
45 ml [3 tablespoons] lemon juice
bay leaf

For the garnish:
watercress sprigs
1 lemon

1 Peel and slice the garlic clove and crush with salt under the blade of a knife.

2 Put the garlic into an earthenware or glass dish, add all the other ingredients for the marinade and stir well.

1 *Chicken with lemon barbecue sauce.* 2 *Country-style chicken is served with bacon and mushrooms.* 3 *Substitute pineapple and chipolata sausages for the bacon and mushrooms for an attractive variation.*

3 Put the chicken pieces in the marinade and spoon the marinade over the chicken. Cover and leave in a cool place for at least 2 hours.

4 Heat the grill to medium heat.

5 Place the chicken pieces skin side down in the grill pan. Cook 12 cm [5″] away from the heat for 15 minutes, basting frequently with the remaining lemon marinade.

6 Turn the chicken skin side up and grill for 10 minutes, basting fre- quently with the lemon marinade.

7 Test the chicken by piercing it with a fine skewer to see that the juices run clear. If the chicken shows signs of overbrowning, turn the heat down. The skin should be crisp when the chicken is cooked.

8 Serve on a hot dish and garnish with lemon quarters and cress.

TANDOORI-STYLE CHICKEN

Frozen chicken can be used for this spicy chicken dish as it is marinated overnight in a yoghurt mixture which tenderizes and flavours the meat. A smaller chicken can be used if it is fresh—the weight given here allows for loss of weight due to thawing and skinning.

If you like a hot dish add 5 ml [¼ teaspoon] chilli powder to the marinade. Powdered ginger is no substitute for fresh root ginger and it is not suitable for this recipe. Fresh root ginger is sometimes available from vegetable markets and always from Indian food shops. Sesame, cumin and coriander seeds, rather than the powdered varieties, are used because the crushed seeds are far more aromatic than powders.

Traditionally, tandoori chicken is red so you can use a few drops of food colouring or spoonfuls of tomato purée to colour the chicken.

SERVES 4
1.6 kg [3½ lb] chicken or 4 chicken portions
salt and pepper
30 ml [2 tablespoons] butter
15 ml [1 tablespoon] le.non juice

For the .narinade:
40 g [1½ oz] fresh ginger
2 garlic cloves
125 ml [4 fl oz] yoghurt
5 ml [1 teaspoon] sesame seeds

Rôtisseries are useful for controlled and even grilling whether for succulent whole chickens or exotic kebabs.

5 ml [1 teaspoon] coriander seeds
5 ml [1 teaspoon] cumin seeds
2.5 ml [½ teaspoon] red food colouring or 30 ml [2 tablespoons] tomato purée

For the garnish:
2 lemons
fresh coriander leaves or watercress

1 Peel and chop the ginger and garlic into very small pieces.

2 Crush the seeds in a mortar with a pestle or with a rolling pin in a small plastic bag.

3 Mix together the yoghurt, sesame, coriander and cumin seeds, ginger, garlic and red colouring or tomato purée.

4 If using a whole chicken, halve it by cutting along the breastbone. Open the chicken and cut along the backbone. Remove the backbone and cut the chicken into quarters.

5 Remove the skin and fat from the chicken portions and, using a sharp knife, make 3 or 4 incisions in the flesh of each portion.

6 Place the chicken pieces in a glass or earthenware dish and spoon the

If using frozen chicken for Tandoori-style chicken allow for weight loss due to defrosting and skinning.

marinade over. Cover and leave for 8 hours, turning occasionally and spooning over the marinade.

7 Heat the grill to medium heat.

8 Remove chicken from marinade and season with salt and pepper.

9 Remove grid and place chicken pieces in the grill pan with the bony side upwards. Pour over the lemon juice, dot with butter and grill 12 cm [5"] away from heat for 12 minutes, basting it two or three times during this time.

10 Turn over the pieces, baste with the pan juices and grill for 8 minutes, again basting the chicken two or three times. Test with a skewer to see that meat is cooked and tender.

11 Place on a warm serving dish. Garnish with coriander leaves and the lemons cut into wedges and serve. Use cress if no coriander.

ROTISSERIES

In rôtisserie cooking the meat is fixed to a spit which is either a long skewer-like pin which goes right through and out the other side or a pair of long 'forks' to grip the meat from either side. This spit is attached at both ends to a framework and is turned automatically. Heat may be from below or above according to the model used. The meat is then revolved slowly so that each side is in turn exposed directly for cooking. The big advantage of spit roasting or grilling is that all sides are quickly seared to seal in the natural juices. On a conventional grill you must hand-turn the meat several times to

just seal, and then cook it. The meat then continues to cook evenly without burning on any one side.

Lean meat should be lightly brushed with melted butter or oil, after fixing to the spit, to ensure that the outside does not brown too quickly. The meat needs no further basting because as it rolls the fat is distributed over the surface. Flavourings, such as herbs, in the cavity of a chicken are also distributed. It is an ideal method for cooking fatty meat if the heat is on top, as all excess fat drips away.

Most rôtisserie models come with a choice of spits. A single spit may be used with a chicken trussed as for roasting—or even two chickens with larger models. Several small game birds can be spit-roasted in a row, or boned and rolled roast meat. Some models have revolving baskets. Several spits can be used simultaneously to cook kebabs.

Barbecues burning both charcoal and gas are available with automatic spits fitted to them. Meat thus cooked is really grilled. Rôtisserie cooking is, in effect, a modern method of spit roasting—the ancient way of cooking meat over an open fire.

Electric models are available and these have heating elements at the top. Because there is a door which is shut, creating an enclosed, heated space, meat cooked in these is as much roasted as grilled. They have the advantage of a time switch, so there is no risk of the meat overcooking if you forget it. Without the spits they can also be used as small ovens—they heat quickly and are economical on electricity—or instead of a conventional grill for browning dishes finished off with cheese, breadcrumbs and other gratin toppings.

13

Perfect poultry

A good cook will roast a chicken so that it has a golden crisp skin and juicy flesh—a simple but real treat. To get these perfect results requires time and care. Because chicken meat is dry thoughtless roasting can easily reduce it to a tasteless, sawdusty texture. Here we describe the preparation, stuffing and roasting needed to produce a golden, succulent chicken and show you how to carve economically.

CHOOSING CHICKEN FOR ROASTING

There's an old saying 'choose the bird that roosts next to the cockerel', and although it is no longer possible to follow this sage advice literally, we can still pick out the plumpest bird, which is the one the cockerel would have singled out! Other signs of youth, such as a pliable tip to the breastbone and a thin skin, are no longer relevant as all chickens sold for roasting are under three months old.

Since chicken meat is lean, it is worth looking for a bird with a thin layer of fat beneath the skin. This fat helps to keep the bird succulent when cooking. You will only find it on larger birds.

All types and sizes of chicken (as described in detail on pages 1 – 4) are young and tender enough to be roasted. The bird you cannot roast is one labelled 'boiling fowl'. This is usually an old and fairly tough bird that has reached the end of its useful life as an egg producer.

Capon

This is a young cockerel treated by injection and then specially fattened for the table. Very few capons are reared nowadays so you may have difficulty finding one. Capons weigh between 2-3.6 kg [4½-8 lb] which is ideal when cooking for a large number of people. Prepare and cook the capon in the same way as a chicken, with the same stuffings and sauces.

INITIAL PREPARATION

Chicken is perishable and must therefore be stored carefully. Remove the butcher's wrapping and put the chicken on a plate. If the giblets are in a bag inside the bird, remove them and store separately. Cover the chicken only lightly with greaseproof

paper or kitchen foil, to allow a little circulation of air. Store it in the coldest part of the refrigerator at the top under the ice compartment.

It is most important to thaw frozen birds before cooking (see on pages 4–5), otherwise the centre may still be raw at the end of cooking time. Fresh or defrosted chickens should be removed from the refrigerator three quarters of an hour before cooking to bring the meat to room temperature. If the chicken is put into the oven straight from the refrigerator because of some emergency, allow an extra 20-30 minutes cooking time.

Most poultry is sold ready for cooking. But there are some preparations specific to roasting chicken which are as necessary to successful appearance and taste as actual roasting.

Look carefully at the bird's skin. If there are any unsightly stubbles where the bases of the feathers are still sticking in the skin remove them. Raise the skin at the point where the stubble occurs and grasp each stubble in turn between your thumb and a round-bladed knife, and tug sharply.

Rinse out the bird's body cavity by holding the tail end under a running tap. Lift the skin of the neck flap, so water runs through the bird. Drain the chicken thoroughly. Then pat dry inside and outside with kitchen paper. This is very important because if the chicken is left wet it will not acquire an attractively brown skin in the oven.

Season the inside of the bird. This is most important as flavours permeate more readily through the inner cavity walls than through the exterior skin.

Stand the bird up and grind salt and pepper into the body cavity through the tail end. You can use salt as well as pepper because there are no cut surfaces to bleed if salted. Chicken, being a white meat, can be salted before cooking.

It is a good idea to insert a moisture-creating ingredient, such as an apple, onion or lemon, inside the bird, as well as flavourings such as herbs or spices and garlic. A dessert apple, onion or lemon also adds a subtle flavour, and gives off juice as it cooks, which helps to keep this lean meat succulent and prevents it from drying out. Discard these additions before serving.

Step-by-step to stuffing a chicken

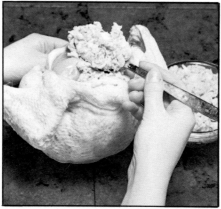

1 Stand bird up with its back to you. Open neck by holding skin back against the breast. Loosely pack the stuffing under the neck skin.

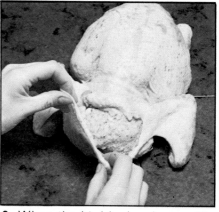

2 When the bird looks plump without being stretched, lay it breast side down. Fold neck skin over the back to enclose stuffing.

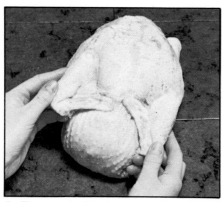

3 The neck skin is secured and held in position on the back of the bird by folding the wing tips over it on each side.

OR fasten the skin 'stitching' it to the back of the chicken with a small poultry skewer (which is removed when serving).

A walnut-sized piece of butter mashed together with salt, pepper and herbs is a valuable addition to the body cavity. The buttery juices can be used for the gravy at the end of cooking.

NON-STUFFY STUFFINGS

Stuffing the bird is another way of adding both moisture and flavour to the meat. A well-chosen stuffing can be the making of a simple roast chicken. It is also economical because it makes the meal more substantial.

Choose ingredients that will provide a stimulating contrast in flavour and texture. Stuffing can add the richness that lean poultry meat lacks. Mild bacon, bacon fat, butter, minced pork and pork sausage meat are all very suitable ingredients for stuffings.

Another important function of a stuffing is to help maintain the bird's moisture by generating steam during cooking. For this reason, stuffings themselves need to be fairly moist and should not be packed tightly but loosely into the neck end of the bird. Avoid stuffing the body cavity as this obstructs the circulation of heat (if you do increase the cooking time).

Although stuffings can be made the day before and refrigerated, they should not be put into the bird until shortly before cooking. The stuffing must be cold, or at least cool, when put into the bird. The quantities given in the recipes are sufficient for stuffing a 1.4-1.8 kg [3-4 lb] chicken. If there is too much stuffing for the neck cavity, the remainder can be cooked separately in a small covered dish on the shelf beneath the bird for the last 30-40 minutes of roasting time.

APRICOT AND HAZELNUT STUFFING

This is an unusual stuffing made with fruit and nuts. Allow the stuffing to cool before inserting it into the bird.

STUFFS 1.4-1.8 KG [3-4 LB] CHICKEN
75 g [3 oz] dried apricots
50 g [2 oz] onion
1 celery stick
40 g [1½ oz] butter
25 g [1 oz] shelled hazelnuts
50 g [2 oz] white bread
2.5 ml [½ teaspoon] finely grated lemon zest
salt
freshly ground black pepper

1 Put the apricots in a bowl and pour over enough boiling water to just cover. Leave to stand while preparing the other ingredients.

2 Peel and finely chop the onion. Wash and chop the celery.

3 Melt the butter in a medium-sized saucepan. Gently fry the onion and celery until soft, but not brown.

4 Meanwhile roughly chop the hazelnuts. Drain and chop the apricots, reserving the liquid.

5 Make the breadcrumbs by grating on a coarse grater. With the pan off the heat add the crumbs to the pan. Add hazelnuts, apricots and lemon zest, with salt and pepper to taste.

6 Mix thoroughly. The apricots should provide enough moisture to bind the stuffing loosely. If the mixture seems too dry to bind, add a little of the water in which the apricots were soaked.

SAUSAGE MEAT AND APPLE STUFFING

This is a quick stuffing to make and must be used immediately before the apple has time to discolour.

STUFFS 1.4-1.8 KG [3-4 LB] CHICKEN
1 cooking apple
225 g [8 oz] pork sausage meat
10 ml [2 teaspoons] dried herbs
salt and black pepper

1 Peel, core and chop the apple.

2 Put the sausage meat, herbs and seasoning into a bowl. Add the apple and mix thoroughly.

3 Use the stuffing for the neck cavity of a bird or cook in a dish underneath the roast for 30-40 minutes.

THREE HERBS STUFFING

This is a traditional parsley and lemon-flavoured stuffing with the addition of marjoram to give it an interesting new flavour. The stuffing should be crumbly in texture and very green.

STUFFS 1.4-1.8 KG [3-4 LB] CHICKEN
45 ml [3 tablespoons] fresh parsley leaves
15 ml [1 tablespoon] fresh marjoram leaves or 5 ml [1 teaspoon] dried marjoram
5 ml [1 teaspoon] fresh lemon thyme leaves or 1.5 ml [¼ teaspoon] dried thyme
1.5 ml [¼ teaspoon] grated lemon zest.
50 g [2 oz] white bread
40 g [1½ oz] butter
salt and pepper

1 Finely chop all the fresh herbs.

2 Make the breadcrumbs by grating on a coarse grater.

3 Melt the butter in a small saucepan.

4 With the pan off the heat, stir the breadcrumbs and herbs into the butter and season to taste.

BACON AND CELERY STUFFING

This stuffing uses the chicken liver that comes with the bird. The stuffing is cooked first so allow it to cool before using it.

STUFFS 1.4-1.8 KG [3-4 LB] CHICKEN
2 rashers smoked streaky bacon
2 small celery sticks
40 g [1½ oz] butter
1 chicken liver
50 g [2 oz] white bread
salt and pepper to taste

1 Remove the bacon rinds and cut the bacon rashers into pieces.

2 Wash the celery, split the sticks lengthways into 2 (or 3 pieces if broad). Cut into 1.2 cm [½"] dice.

3 Melt the butter in a small saucepan. Add the bacon and celery and fry, covered, for 5 minutes.

4 Wash and then blot the liver with kitchen paper. Remove any stringy parts. Chop and add to the pan.

5 Stir in the breadcrumbs and season to taste.

6 Allow the stuffing to cool then stuff into neck cavity of a chicken.

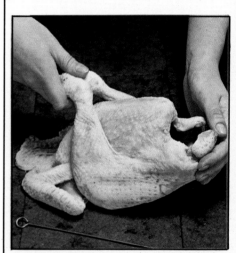

1 Laying the bird on its back lift the legs and pull them back towards the neck.

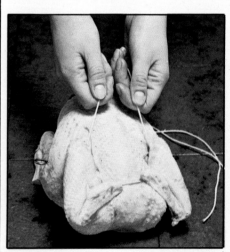

5 Cut a long piece of thin string and centre it, whilst placing it under the wings.

TRUSSING A CHICKEN

These days chickens and capons are usually sold drawn and trussed ready for the oven. Sometimes, however, you may need to truss a bird at home, or retruss one after stuffing it. The purpose of trussing is simply to hold the bird in a compact shape during cooking, so that it browns evenly and looks attractive when served. The joints of an untrussed bird would spread out in the oven and be very untidy. Parts like wing tips may also burn.

Trussing after stuffing is done either with a trussing needle, threaded with fine string, or very simply with a skewer and string as shown in detail in the step-by-step pictures below.

PRECAUTIONS AGAINST DRYING OUT

Chicken is a very lean meat and precautions both before and during roasting are essential to prevent it from drying out. The breast meat is especially susceptible to drying as it has no natural fat and, being at the top of the chicken, is more exposed to the heat.

The most usual precaution is to bard the breast. The breast is completely covered with thin rashers of mild fatty bacon, such as streaky, which are laid across it covering the top of the drumsticks as well. The barding bacon is removed just before the end of cooking to allow the breast to brown before serving. The bacon may be reserved and crumbled into the gravy if you wish.

Another method is to cover the breast loosely with a double thickness of well-buttered greaseproof paper, a butter wrapper, or buttered foil. The paper is discarded 20 minutes before the cooking time is up. The chicken should be painted all over with a generous coating of oil or softened butter.

A method much practised in France, is to rub the bird all over with softened butter and to roast it breast downwards for the major part of cooking time. This method encourages the juices to run down into the breast meat and keeps it beautifully succulent. The bird is then reversed, breast upwards, for the last 20 minutes of cooking. Baste it

Step-by-step to trussing a chicken

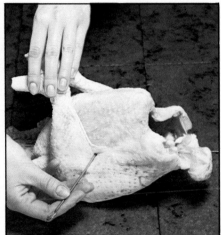

2 Pass a metal skewer through the body meat, inserting it in the angle of the thigh and drumstick.

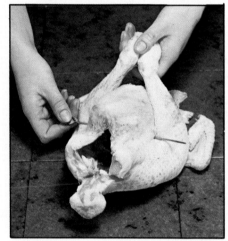

3 Push the skewer through the bird so that it emerges in the corresponding place on the other side.

4 Turn bird on to its breast. Fold the wing tips across the back to hold the neck skin in position.

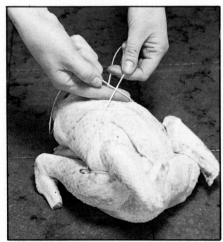

6 Draw the ends of string under, up and over the skewer ends then cross them over the bird's back.

7 Turn the bird on to its back. Twist the string around the leg ends then under the parson's nose.

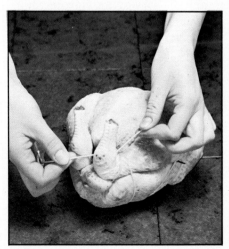

8 Tie the two ends of the string securely so that the legs and tail are firmly held together.

thoroughly to allow the skin to brown. Baste again after 10 minutes and complete cooking time. The chicken should be succulent and tender.

CAREFUL ROASTING
The following simple rules will help you achieve a successful roast—crisp and golden outside, succulent within.

Always heat the oven so that it is at the required temperature when the bird is put into it. A fairly hot oven, 190°C[375°F] gas mark 5 is effective and economical for a small bird. A slightly lower temperature of 180°C [350°F] gas mark 4 is used for a larger bird to ensure that it is cooked all the way through. If the body cavity is stuffed, allow an extra 20-30 minutes.

For a crisp skin, rub salt all over with your fingers, working it well into the cracks. The oil or butter may then be painted on with a brush afterwards.

Unless roasting in the French way, place the chicken on a rack, breast side upwards. There is no need to put fat in the tin unless the giblets are used. If bacon is used for barding, this will make a certain amount of fat. The moisturizing ingredients inside the bird, whether butter or fruit or vegetable, will also make a certain amount of juice. This can be used for basting the bird in the last 20 minutes to ensure a crisp, golden skin.

If the breast is to be covered by foil or paper, this must be well-buttered with 15 g [½ oz] of butter or margarine. It is wise also to put a little butter inside the bird to create enough fat for basting. Baste two or three times during the last 20 minutes when the chicken is uncovered.

The French method
This method of roasting uses more fat and gives the chicken a crisp golden skin all over in much the same fashion as a rôtisserie-cooked chicken. It takes longer than the English method of roasting given above, because frequent basting and turning of the bird are necessary.

Butter is always inserted in the bird's cavity after seasoning. Herbs may also be added, the most common one being tarragon. The outside of the bird is rubbed over with salt and pepper and then generously brushed all over with a mixture of butter and oil or butter and lemon juice.

CHICKEN ROASTING TIMES
Times for cooking fully thawed, room-temperature birds, stuffed at the neck end only.*

oven-ready weight	number of servings	oven temperature	cooking time
1 kg [2 lb]	2-3	190°C [375°F] gas mark 5	1 hour
1.4 kg [3 lb]	4	190°C [375°F] gas mark 5	1 hr 20 mins
1.8 kg [4 lb]	5-6	190°C [375°F] gas mark 5	1 hr 40 mins
2.25 kg [5 lb]	7-8	190°C [375°F] gas mark 5	2 hours
2.7 kg [6 lb]	8-9	180°C [350°F] gas mark 4	2 hrs 15 mins
3.2 kg [7 lb]	10	180°C [350°F] gas mark 4	2 hrs 30 mins
3.6 kg [8 lb]	12	180°C [350°F] gas mark 4	2 hrs 45 mins

*If the body cavity contains stuffing, allow an extra 20-30 minutes cooking time.

THE GIBLETS
The giblets contribute a considerable amount of flavour to a chicken and should never be discarded. They consist of the neck, gizzard, heart and liver. When you buy an oven-ready bird the giblets are usually wrapped separately and tucked inside the body cavity. As soon as you get a fresh bird home or, if frozen, as soon as it has thawed, remove the giblets from their wrapping and wash them under the cold tap. Check that the liver is free of gall. Look for any area that is stained green and cut away and discard it as gall is very bitter. Remove any thick yellow skin remaining on the gizzard.

●Make stock from the giblets. Put all the washed giblets except the liver, into a small saucepan. Add a slice or two of onion, carrot and celery, a small bay leaf, 3 peppercorns, 1.5 ml [¼ teaspoon] salt, and 250 ml [½ pt] of water. Bring to the boil, cover, and simmer for 30 minutes. Cool, strain and use the stock for the gravy.

●Add the cooked heart, gizzard and neck meat, all finely chopped, to the stuffing.
●Cook the washed giblets, excepting the liver, in the roasting tin beneath the chicken. You will need to add 15 ml [1 tablespoon] of fat to the roasting tin. This is a simple way of ensuring that their flavour will enrich the gravy.
●The raw liver can be chopped and added to the stuffing or roasted beside the bird for the last 15 minutes of cooking time. Remember to baste it well. It can also be used to make liver and bacon rolls.
●If you can't use the giblets immediately, freeze them until you have collected enough to make a rich giblet soup.
●Cooked chicken carcasses can be frozen for making stock later, but be sure to freeze them promptly while they are still fresh.
●Freeze the livers separately so they can be used for a special omelette filling or for making a pâté.

The chicken is not placed upon a rack or trivet but laid in the pan on one side of its breast. Be sure that the thigh in the highest position is well buttered. After 25 minutes the chicken is turned on to the other breast. Baste all the upper surface thoroughly with the pan juices. Finally after 25 minutes, the chicken is turned on to its back and the breast is thoroughly basted for browning.

To test when a chicken is cooked
Undercooked chicken is slimy and unpleasant to eat, pink at the thickest part round the thigh joints and it gives off a pink juice when pierced. It can also be a health hazard. It is important to cook chicken thoroughly, until a meat thermometer inserted into the fleshiest part of the thigh registers 80-82°C [175-180°F].

Step-by-step to roasting chicken

1 Remove the bird from refrigerator to reach room temperature. Weigh and calculate the cooking time.

2 Sprinkle cavity liberally with salt and black pepper. Insert stuffing or moisturizing ingredients.

3 Place chicken, breast upwards, on a rack or trivet in a roasting tin. The juices drain into the tin.

4 Bard or cover the chicken breast and thigh tops with thin rashers of bacon. Roast the chicken.

5 Remove and discard bacon 20 minutes before cooking ends, so that the skin can crisp.

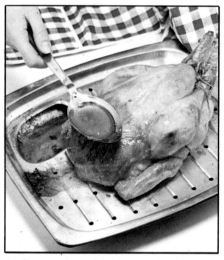

6 Baste the chicken with the pan juices two or three times to moisten and help crisp the skin.

7 Test the chicken by piercing it with a skewer. If the juices run clear the chicken is ready.

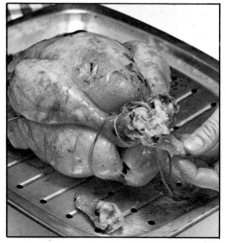

8 Twist the leg shanks to remove them. Remove any trussing string and the skewers if present.

9 As you lift the bird to transfer it, tilt it so that the juices run from the tail end into the pan.

An alternative reliable test is to pierce the chicken deeply in the thigh with a skewer and note the colour of the juices that run from it. When fully cooked the juices will be colourless or yellowish. If they are pink, return the roast to the oven and continue cooking a little longer before testing again.

Dishing up

Choose a serving dish large enough to accommodate the chicken and any garnishes such as bacon rolls, chipolatas or watercress. There should also be plenty of room for the chicken joints as the carver separates them from the carcass. It makes carving more difficult if the plate is crowded.

As you lift the bird to place it on the warmed serving dish, tilt the tail end (the end with the parson's nose) downward for a few seconds. The juices in the body of the bird will then drain into the roasting pan and improve the gravy.

Always leave the chicken to rest for ten minutes before carving, to allow the meat to set. This also gives you time to make the gravy.

Cut the trussing string and pull away from the bird. Remove the skewer if there is one. Using a piece of kitchen paper to keep your fingers clean, twist off the leg shanks, which are inedible and unsightly. Before serving, if you wish, you can use a cutlet frill to cover the ends of the legs, but this is not essential.

Cooked garnishes are then arranged round the dish. Salad garnishes must be added at the very last moment before serving.

CARVING A CHICKEN OR CAPON

It is easy to make a professional job of carving a chicken or capon. The flesh is very tender, and, once you have mastered the art of finding and severing the ball and socket thigh joint, there are no real problems.

Step-by-step to carving a large chicken

1 Drive the fork into the bird to hold it firmly and carve off the right leg and thigh.

2 Holding the knuckle joint, sever the thigh from the drumstick through the ball and socket joint.

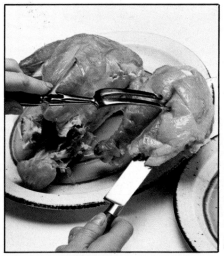

3 Turn the dish and carve the left side. Each of the four leg pieces with breast meat makes a portion.

5 Again turn the dish, so that the wishbone is to your right. Insert knife in front of breastbone.

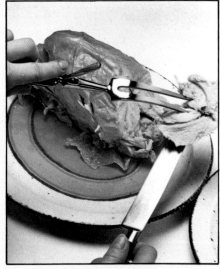

6 Cut down following curve of wishbone. With breast meat this makes one portion.

7 With front end facing you, carve the breast into thin slices using downward strokes of the knife.

The method of carving a large chicken or a capon is an extension of that used for a small bird, so if possible practise on a small bird first. As well as a sharp knife, and a carving fork with a finger guard, you will need a spoon for serving a crumbly stuffing. A napkin is also used for holding the leg tip when the thigh and drumstick needs to be divided.

CLASSIC ACCOMPANIMENTS

Classic accompaniments are chicken liver and bacon rolls, pork chipolatas and, of course, bread sauce.

4 Carve each of the wing joints. (Serve with some of the breast meat to make two more portions.)

8 Portions can be made up of breast meat and any remaining meat such as the oyster pieces on the back.

Step-by-step to carving a small chicken

1 The chicken should be allowed to rest before carving in order that the meat can firm up.

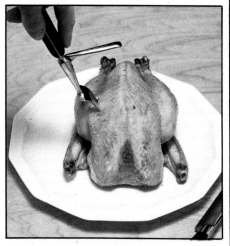

2 With the wishbone facing you, hold the bird firmly in place by driving the fork into left side.

3 Cut through the skin and around the right leg joint to free the leg from the body of the chicken.

4 Starting at the wishbone end of the breastbone, hold the knife close against the carcass.

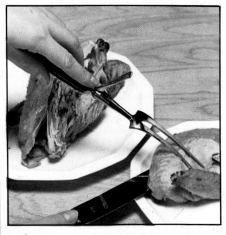

5 Carve away the whole breast and wing in one piece so that you have the second portion.

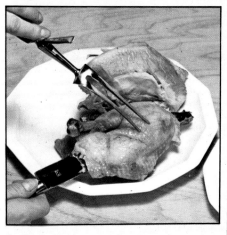

6 Repeat the carving on the other side until the bird is divided into four portions.

BREAD SAUCE

This essentially English sauce adds both piquant flavour and contrast to the texture of the chicken. The secret of well-flavoured bread sauce depends on a long enough infusion of the onion and spices in the milk to impart a really distinctive flavour. The consistency should be that of thick cream, neither thin nor stiff.

SERVES 6
**1 small onion
2 cloves
250 ml [½ pt] milk
4 peppercorns
1 small blade mace
1 bay leaf
50 g [2 oz] stale white bread
salt
25 g [1 oz] butter or 15 ml
[1 tablespoon] cream**

1 Peel and slice the onion, stud it with the cloves.

2 Put the milk into a small saucepan and add the studded onion, peppercorns, mace and bay leaf.

3 Bring slowly to boiling point. Remove the pan from the heat, cover it and leave in a warm place to infuse for at least 30 minutes, preferably longer.

4 Make the breadcrumbs by grating the bread on a coarse grater.

5 Strain the milk and discard the onion, herbs and spices. Return the milk to the saucepan and stir in the breadcrumbs.

6 Leave to stand for 15 minutes while the crumbs absorb the milk.

7 Reheat gently before serving, add salt to taste and stir in the butter or cream.

FRENCH ROAST CHICKEN

The French method of open roasting a small chicken differs from the English in that the bird is cooked initially on its side and needs turning and basting. It is usually cooked without a stuffing, and is invariably served with a crisp green salad. Traditionally the quantity of gravy is very small, but is very well flavoured. Potato crisps can be warmed through in the oven and used as a garnish.

SERVES 4
**1.4 kg [3 lb] chicken
salt and pepper
50 g [2 oz] butter
sprigs of fresh or dried herbs,
   such as rosemary, lemon
   thyme or tarragon
10 ml [2 teaspoons] oil
giblet stock**

1 Heat the oven to 190°C [375°F] gas mark 5.

2 Wash, drain and dry the chicken.

3 Mash the salt and pepper into 15 g [½ oz] butter. If you are using dried herbs, these may be added to the butter. Put the butter and any fresh herbs into the body cavity. Retruss the bird if necessary.

4 Rub salt and pepper over the chicken skin. Melt the remaining butter with the oil and brush the bird liberally all over.

5 Rest the bird on one side of its breast in a roasting tin just large enough to hold it comfortably. Roast in the centre of the oven for 25 minutes.

6 Turn the bird on the other side, baste with the butter and oil, and roast for another 25 minutes.

7 Meanwhile prepare the giblet stock and leave to simmer.

8 Turn the chicken breast upwards and baste with the remaining butter and oil or drippings in tin.

9 Fifteen minutes before the end of cooking time, baste the chicken with the juices that have collected in the roasting tin.

10 Test if the chicken is cooked by piercing the thigh with a skewer. The juices should be colourless.

11 Tilt the bird to drain the juices from the body cavity into the roasting tin.

12 Transfer the chicken to a large warm serving dish. Remove the trussings, skewers and leg shanks and keep warm.

13 Tilt the roasting tin and pour off any surplus fat, leaving the drippings behind. Strain the giblet stock into the tin.

14 Bring to the boil over medium heat. Stir and scrape round the pan to release the scrapings from the bottom of the tin.

15 Simmer for 5 minutes until stock has reduced. Check the seasoning. Serve in a warm sauce-boat.

TRADITIONAL ROAST CHICKEN

A large chicken, or a capon, is the bird to choose when you plan to spend time preparing all the delicious trimmings. Instead of expensive bacon for barding, cover the bird with foil, and reserve the bacon for rolls to eat with the bird. It helps to prepare the breadcrumbs for stuffing and sauce in advance.

SERVES 7-8
**2.25 kg [5 lb] roasting chicken
25 g [1 oz] butter
three herb stuffing (or any other
   stuffing)
salt and pepper
small dessert apple
giblet stock
the chicken liver
bread sauce
4 rashers streaky bacon
225 g [½ lb] pork chipolatas**

**For the garnish:
a few sprigs of watercress**

The French roast a chicken by placing it on its side initially, turning and basting it and then completing roasting time in the usual position.

1 Remove the butter from the refrigerator. Uncover and leave to come to room temperature.

2 Prepare the stuffing and leave to cool.

3 Heat the oven to 190°C [375°F] gas mark 5.

4 Prepare, wash, drain and thoroughly dry the chicken. Sprinkle the body cavity and the skin with salt and pepper.

5 Peel the dessert apple and put it into the body cavity.

6 Fill the neck end of the bird with the stuffing, fold the skin over the back and secure with wing tips or poultry skewer. Retruss the bird if necessary.

7 Spread some of the butter on a piece of foil to cover the breast, then spread the rest all over the chicken.

8 Stand the chicken on a rack in a roasting tin and cover the breast loosely with the buttered foil. Roast in the centre of the oven for a total of 2 hours.

9 Meanwhile prepare the giblet stock (reserving the liver). Infuse the milk for the bread sauce.

10 Cut the rinds off the bacon, stretch the rashers with a knife, and cut in half. Place a portion of chicken liver on each piece of bacon, roll up and impale on a small skewer.

11 Separate the chipolatas and put in a lightly greased ovenproof dish.

12 Half an hour before the end of roasting time discard the foil and baste the chicken with the pan juices. Put the dish of chipolatas, uncovered, on the shelf beneath the bird.

13 Quarter of an hour before roasting time is up, baste the bird again and put the liver and bacon rolls on roasting tin base.

14 Finish making the bread sauce. Put it into a sauce-boat or serving bowl and keep warm.

15 Test if the bird is cooked by piercing the thigh with a skewer. If the juices are colourless remove the chicken from the oven.

16 Tilt the chicken to drain the juices from the body cavity into the roasting tin.

17 Place the bird on a heated serving dish. Remove the trussing strings and the skewer. Break off the leg shanks.

18 Arrange the chipolatas and bacon rolls round the chicken and keep warm.

19 Tilt the roasting tin and skim off the surface fat. Strain the giblet stock into the roasting tin. Put the tin over a medium heat and bring to the boil, stirring. Simmer for 5 minutes until the quantity of liquid has reduced. Check seasoning and transfer to a sauce-boat.

20 Just before serving, garnish the tail end of the bird with watercress.

ROAST TARRAGON CHICKEN

◻◻ *Chicken, cream and fresh tarragon are one of the great flavour combinations for the summer months. This chicken is roasted by the French method. Dried tarragon has its uses for flavouring but for this simple recipe fresh tarragon is essential.*

New potatoes, French beans and buttered baby carrots would make a perfect accompaniment.

SERVES 4
1 oven ready chicken weighing 1.4 kg [3 lb]
50 g [2 oz] butter at room temperature
salt and ground black pepper
3 tablespoons fresh tarragon leaves
1 small clove garlic
150 ml [¼ pt] thin cream
5 ml [1 teaspoon] flour
15 ml [1 tablespoon] cold chicken stock

The pineapple rings left over from the stuffing are used as a garnish.

1 Remove the butter from the refrigerator to bring it to room temperature.

2 Heat the oven to 190°C [375°F] gas mark 5.

3 Wash and dry the chicken. Sprinkle the body cavity with salt and pepper and rub salt over the skin.

4 Chop the tarragon leaves roughly. Peel and crush the garlic. Reserve half the butter then cream 25 g [1 oz] with the garlic. Add half the tarragon leaves. Put this mixture into the body cavity of the bird.

5 Truss the chicken if necessary, then spread it all over with the remaining softened butter.

6 Place the bird on one side of its breast in a roasting tin just large enough to hold it comfortably. Roast in the centre of the oven for 25 minutes.

7 Turn the chicken on to its other breast and baste it thoroughly. Roast for 25 minutes.

8 Finally turn the chicken breast upwards. Baste it with the pan drippings and roast for another 25 minutes basting it two or three times.

9 Test the chicken, by piercing with a skewer. The juices should be colourless.

24

10 Tilt the chicken so that the juices run into the pan, then transfer the bird to a warmed serving dish. Remove the trussing strings, skewer and the leg shanks. Keep warm.

11 Add the cream and the rest of the chopped tarragon to the buttery juices in the roasting tin. Heat gently over a low heat. Stir round the pan with a wooden spoon to release the scrapings.

12 Put the flour in a small bowl and add the cold stock. Stir to a smooth paste.

13 Spoon a little of the hot cream on to the flour paste and incorporate it.

14 Transfer the flour paste back to the roasting tin off the heat. Stir to incorporate.

15 Return the baking tin to a gentle heat and bring to the boil, whisking continually with a small wire whisk. Simmer gently for 2-3 minutes to cook the flour. Check the seasonings.

16 Joint the chicken and pour a little of the sauce over it. Serve the rest in a sauce-boat.

ROAST CHICKEN WITH PINEAPPLE WALNUT STUFFING

Trying a new stuffing is a good way of ringing the changes on roast chicken. The flavours and textures of both pineapple and walnuts are in pleasant contrast with chicken, but it is essential to use top quality canned pineapple. The stock can be made with half a bouillon cube as the giblets are roasted in the tin with the chicken and will add their flavour at the end.

SERVES 4
**1.4 kg [3 lb] chicken with giblets
salt and pepper
25 g [1 oz] butter
250 ml [½ pt] stock**

**For the stuffing:
350 g [12 oz] canned pineapple
  rings
50 g [2 oz] walnuts, chopped
40 g [1½ oz] butter
50 g [2 oz] dry white
  breadcrumbs**

**1 level teaspoon salt
half a lemon**

**For the garnish:
a few walnut halves
watercress**

· 1 To make the stuffing, drain the pineapple rings, weigh out 100 g [4 oz] and chop them, reserving the rest for the garnish.

2 Chop the walnuts and grate the zest from the half lemon.

3 Melt the butter for the stuffing in a small saucepan, add the breadcrumbs and stir and cook for a minute or so.

4 Stir the chopped pineapple, chopped walnuts, salt, lemon zest and add enough pineapple juice to give the stuffing a fairly moist consistency.

5 Heat the oven to 190°C [375°F] gas mark 5.

6 Wash, drain and dry the chicken.

7 Sprinkle the body cavity with salt and pepper, and rub well into the skin. Insert 12 g [½ oz] of butter into the cavity.

8 Fill the neck end of the bird with the stuffing and retruss the bird.

9 Soften the remaining 12 g [½ oz] butter. Use some of it to grease a piece of kitchen foil. Spread the rest of the butter all over the bird. Cover the breast with foil.

10 Put the giblets, but not the liver, in the bottom of the roasting tin, and stand the chicken, breast up, on a rack, over them.

11 Cook in the centre of the oven for 1 hour.

12 Remove the foil, baste the bird with the pan drippings, and put the liver in the tin beside the bird and baste it. Cook for another 20 minutes.

13 Test the chicken by piercing the thigh with a skewer. The juices should be colourless.

14 Tilt the chicken to drain the juices into the roasting tin and transfer the chicken to a warmed serving dish. Remove the trussing strings and break off the leg shanks.

15 Add the stock to the roasting tin and bring to the boil, stirring and scraping to release the sediment from the bottom of the tin. Simmer for 2-3 minutes until slightly reduced.

16 Check the seasonings then strain the sauce into a sauce-boat and discard the giblets.

17 Halve the remaining pineapple rings, arrange them around the chicken, topping each half with a walnut. Tuck a few sprigs of watercress between the chicken legs.

Talking turkey

Gone are the days when only the rich ate turkey, and even they only once a year. Today's turkeys are such good value for money, they could well take the place of the traditional Sunday roast. Turkey is easy to roast and can be given extra flavour with tasty stuffings and sauces to make good value family meals the whole year round.

Turkey has been favourite fare for festive occasions since the time of the first Queen Elizabeth. Legend has it that when Columbus sailed the ocean blue, in the year of 1492, one of the things he brought back with him was the turkey. Because it was rare, turkey was looked on as a delicacy, though contemporary accounts suggest that the birds of those times were stringy compared to the plump, well-fed fowl that we know. Because turkey was a delicacy, it became linked with special days, such as Christmas and Thanksgiving. The fact that turkeys were difficult to rear and rather expensive also meant that roast turkey could not be served too often.

Modern rearing techniques which revolutionized our chicken-eating habits have now done the same for turkeys. No longer are we forced to face an 11.3 kg [25 lb] monster which will last for weeks. Turkeys today are specially bred to mature at different stages and are now available weighing from 2.2 kg [5 lb]— just right for a family Sunday lunch or a special

dinner. Modern turkeys are excellent value for money and if cooked and carved correctly, can prove cheaper than more everyday meats.

CHOOSING A TURKEY

There are several different types of roasting turkey available. With each type the points to look for are a plump breast and white flesh; smooth black legs indicate that the bird is young and therefore tender.

When considering what type of turkey to buy, consider also the size of the bird and the size of your oven.

New York dressed and traditional farm fresh

These are the fresh birds seen hanging in poulterers' windows at Christmas, plucked, but with the head and feet still attached. Fresh birds are still the choice of traditionalists who claim that they have a better flavour than chilled and frozen birds. Turkey producers, however,

claim that there is now no difference between the flavours of fresh, chilled and frozen turkeys. When buying a New York dressed bird, you pay for the weight of the head, feet and innards as well as the edible parts of the bird. It is estimated that these can weigh as much as 1.4 kg [3 lb]. New York dressed birds are more expensive per 450 g [1 lb] than other birds because the butcher has to dehead and eviscerate at the point of sale, unlike prepared birds which can just be handed over the counter. Only the larger birds weighing from 4.5–11.3 kg [10–25 lb] are sold New York dressed.

Chilled turkeys

Chilled turkeys are eviscerated and dressed for the oven on the farm and then air chilled rather than frozen. There is no intake of water in this process, unlike the deep-freezing process. Chilled birds are slightly more expensive than frozen and have the advantage that there is no thawing time to consider. They are available in sizes from 2.2–11.3 [5–25 lb].

Chilled birds are usually sold in chain stores, bagged and labelled with the giblets in a separate bag inside.

Frozen turkeys

The cheapness and ready availability of frozen turkeys have largely been responsible for moving the turkey away from the Christmas dinner table to other, less festive, times of the year. Frozen turkeys are sold oven ready with the giblets in a little bag inside. In the freezing process, there is quite a large intake of water which will add about 5% to the weight of the bird. Lengthy thawing is required to make the bird really tender. Frozen turkeys are available in sizes from 2.2–11.3 kg [5–25 lb].

Turkeys do not necessarily have to be enormous things that won't fit into the oven. Garnished with traditional accompaniments, a small bird is perfectly suitable for a Christmas dinner.

Self-basting turkeys

Self-basting turkeys are frozen birds which have vegetable oil or butter injected under the skin. This keeps the flesh moist during roasting and means that no basting is needed. Once thawed and prepared you literally put the bird in the oven and forget about it. Self-basting birds are slightly more expensive than ordinary frozen birds.

Turkey rolls

Turkey rolls are boneless turkey meat rolled up and are available fresh, chilled and frozen. They are rolls of breast meat only, dark meat (leg) only, or a mixture of breast and dark meat, wrapped in turkey skin or pork fat and tied with string or encased in a meat mesh. They are sold plain or stuffed. They are more expensive per 450 g [1 lb] than whole birds but as there is no waste, the actual price per 450 g [1 lb] of edible flesh works out at about the same as for a whole turkey. Turkey rolls are without doubt the best choice if you want to serve a large number of people with sliced turkey as, being boned, they are very easy to carve. They are particularly good for slicing cold and a 4.5 kg [10 lb] turkey roll would provide enough cold sliced meat for 40 people, working on the catering allowance of 100 g [$\frac{1}{4}$ lb] meat per person.

STORING TURKEY

Fresh turkeys should be stored separately from their giblets, on a plate in the coldest part of the refrigerator. Covered loosely with greaseproof paper, a fresh turkey will keep safely for 2 days. The giblets have a shorter life and should, if possible, be used to make giblet stock for gravy on the day the turkey is bought. Reserve the liver for use in the stuffing if preferred.

Fresh turkey rolls should be stored as for whole birds.

Chilled turkeys should be stored according to the manufacturers' instructions. This varies from processor to processor so read the label carefully.

The same applies to chilled turkey rolls.

Frozen turkeys should be stored in a freezer or star marked frozen-food compartment if not immediately required for thawing.

Frozen turkey rolls should be stored in the same way.

THAWING TIMES FOR TURKEY

Thaw your frozen turkey on a rack over a tray, in the bottom of the refrigerator. Remove wrapping as soon as bird is sufficiently thawed to do so. Remove bag of giblets from the bird as well.

Weight	Thawing Time
2.2–3.6 kg [5–8 lb]	20–36 hours
3.6–5 kg [8–11 lb]	36–42 hours
5–5.9 kg [11–13 lb]	42–48 hours
5.9–9.1 kg [13–20 lb]	48–60 hours
9.1–11.3 kg [20–25 lb]	60–72 hours

TURKEY SIZES

Uncooked weight	No. of servings
2.2 kg [5 lb]	4
2.7 kg [6 lb]	5
3.1 kg [7 lb]	6
3.6 kg [8 lb]	7
4 kg [9 lb]	8
4.5 kg [10 lb]	10
5 kg [11 lb]	12
5.5 kg [12 lb]	13
5.9 kg [13 lb]	15
6.4 kg [14 lb]	17
6.8 kg [15 lb]	19
7.3 kg [16 lb]	20
7.7 kg [17 lb]	22
8.2 kg [18 lb]	24
8.6 kg [19 lb]	26
9.1 kg [20 lb]	28
9.5 kg [21 lb]	30
10.1 kg [22 lb]	32
10.5 kg [23 lb]	34
11 kg [24 lb]	36
11.3 kg [25 lb]	38

THAWING FROZEN TURKEY

Thorough, slow thawing of frozen turkeys and turkey rolls is essential for health and for flavour. They should be thawed in a cool place, where the temperature will not rise above 15°C [59°F]. Turkeys should always be thawed in their plastic wrappings: this helps to prevent drying out. Raise the bird on a rack or grid over a tray into which the water can drip. Never attempt to accelerate the defrosting process by placing the turkey in hot water. This toughens the flesh and can lead to insufficient thawing before cooking. If a turkey is not thawed thoroughly all the way through before cooking, it will not cook right through and the germs which cause food poisoning will not be destroyed. The chart given here indicates thawing times which will ensure your turkey is thoroughly thawed and safe. It is always best to cook the bird as soon as possible once it has been thoroughly thawed. When thawing turkey rolls, follow the manufacturer's instructions as these vary.

The neck cavity of a turkey is stuffed and not the body cavity. Stuffing ingredients can include the turkey liver, sausage meat, mushrooms, nuts, currants, herbs and spices.

HOW MUCH TO BUY

What size turkey you buy depends very much on what you want to do with it. If you want it only for one meal then it is likely that a smaller bird will be the best choice. If you have guests over several days, it would be more economical to buy a larger bird where there is a greater proportion of flesh to bone. The bird could be served roasted first, and then used for a number of réchauffé dishes. If these were made sufficiently varied (turkey pie, croquettes, curry, pilaf are just four you could choose from), your turkey could be used for several meals without anyone tiring of it. A large bird is also the best choice for a party, where it makes a splendid centrepiece.

For a buffet party or an occasion where cold sliced turkey will be served, a turkey roll is a better choice than a whole bird as it is quick and easy to carve and there is no waste.

The chart here is calculated to take into account the weight of the bones and to allow the professional caterer's portion weight of 100 g [¼ lb] meat per person. The weights are for oven-ready, raw, defrosted birds. When buying a New York dressed bird, remember to allow about an extra 1.4 kg [3 lb] for the weight of head, feet and entrails. On frozen birds allow up to 225 g [½ lb] extra for the weight of giblets and water. On chilled birds allow 100 g [¼ lb] for the weight of the giblets. With rolls there is no need to make any allowance as there is no waste, and only minimal water intake as the flesh is so closely packed. When buying a roll, base your calculations on four portions per 450 g [1 lb]. When buying a whole bird, follow the chart given here.

PREPARING FOR ROASTING

First rinse the bird with cold water and pat dry carefully both inside and out. If the inside of the bird is damp

Step-by-step to trussing a turkey

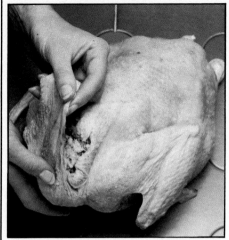

1 Lay the bird breast side down. Make sure the neck skin is flat to the back, enclosing the stuffing.

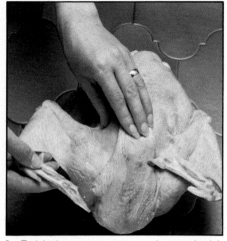

2 Fold the wing tips under to hold the neck skin in place and so that the wings are close to the body.

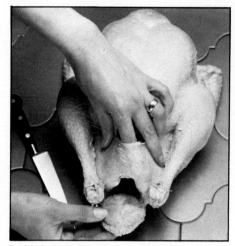

3 Make a slit in the skin above the vent. Push the parson's nose through this slit.

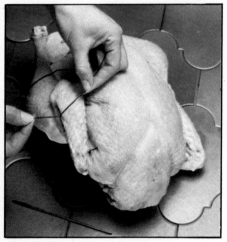

6 Push back through to secure wing tips and neck skin. Bring out at first joint of wing. Tie off.

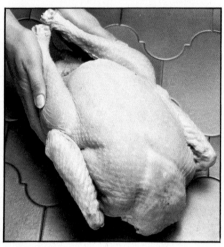

7 Using both hands press the legs to the sides so that the breast is plumped up.

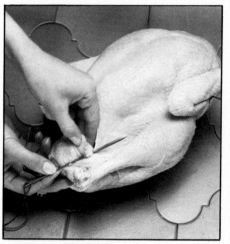

8 Turn bird round and insert the needle in the gristle at the right of the parson's nose. Make a stitch.

when cooking, the flesh will steam and inhibit the roasting. Season the bird liberally inside with salt and freshly ground black pepper. If you are roasting the bird plain without any stuffing, half a lemon and a couple of plump garlic cloves (peeled and left whole) or a sprig of fresh sage, thyme, basil or marjoram placed in the body cavity will delicately flavour the flesh.

If you have bought a fresh New York dressed bird, there may be a few quills remaining where the bird has been plucked. A sharp tug will bring these out without breaking the skin. Chilled and frozen birds are machine plucked and do not have quills left.

If you are roasting a turkey roll, it will be oven ready and there is no need to do any of the above.

Stuffing

You may see in older recipe books that turkeys are stuffed at both ends. This is not really a very good idea as stuffing the cavity can prevent the turkey being properly cooked, leading to an attack of what doctors call 'the Christmas collywobbles'. The neck cavity of a turkey will take quite a large amount of stuffing so there will be no shortage if you only stuff the neck end. As a rough guide, allow 25–40 g [1–1½ oz] of stuffing per 450 g [1 lb] raw oven-ready turkey.

The method is the same as for stuffing a chicken. (See step-by-step to stuffing a chicken on page 15).

The stuffing used should not be put into the bird until shortly before cooking, nor should it be made in advance. The stuffing must be cold,

or at least cool, when put into the bird. Push the prepared stuffing into the neck cavity of the turkey, packing as full as possible. Stuffing mixtures should always be fairly damp and sticky so that they will pack in. When the cavity is full, fold the neck skin over to enclose the stuffing. Fold the wing tips over the skin on each side to hold it in place, or fasten the skin with a small poultry skewer.

If you wish to serve more stuffing than the bird can accommodate, it can be cooked in a greased baking dish covered with foil, on a lower shelf, for the last 30–40 minutes of roasting time.

Trussing

Although some turkeys are sold ready trussed (it usually says so on

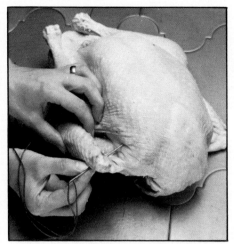

4 Thread a trussing needle with fine string. Insert at second joint of right wing and push into bird.

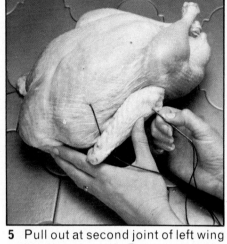

5 Pull out at second joint of left wing leaving an end. Re-insert at the first joint of this wing.

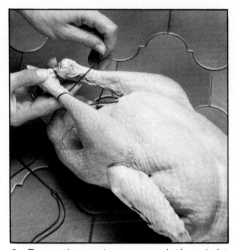

9 Pass the string around the right leg, over the body and over the left leg.

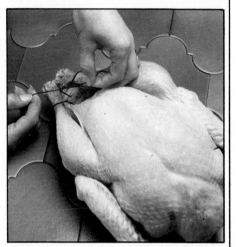

10 Insert again in gristle on left of the parson's nose. Bring under the parson's nose and tie off.

the packet), many are not. Trussing has rather gone out of fashion but for a large bird it is essential, otherwise legs and wings will fly akimbo in the oven and carving will be rather like a tussle with an octopus!

If trussing is new to you, it may well take a few minutes. It is one of those tasks that once familiar can be accomplished in no time. Because turkeys are usually quite large, they should be trussed with a trussing needle and string rather than with a skewer as described for chicken, pages 16–17. The trussing needle used is rather like a large darning needle with an eye big enough to take fine string. Always use natural rather than plastic coated or nylon string for trussing. If you use plastic or nylon string it will melt and ruin the turkey.

STUFFINGS

Stuffing adds flavour to the flesh of turkey and provides a pleasant contrast in texture. Never buy ready-made stuffing mix. It is mostly bread and is flavourless. Much tastier stuffings, which are also economical, can be made quite easily at home. Instructions on how to stuff are given in the section on preparing for roasting.

The stuffings given here are all to fill the neck cavity of a bird weighing 4.5 kg [10 lb]. An easy way to work out how much stuffing you will need is to allow roughly 25–40 g [1–1½ oz] for every 450 g [1 lb] of bird.

Sage and onion stuffing is the classic Christmas stuffing for turkey. It may be made with either fresh or dried sage. Fresh sage gives the stuffing a better flavour, as with any fresh herb. Dried sage can sometimes taste a little musty.

SAUSAGE FORCEMEAT

In the days when turkeys were always stuffed at both ends, the sausage forcemeat went in the neck end. You may, if you wish, stuff the neck end with another stuffing and cook this forcemeat separately. One of the traditonal ways to serve forcemeat is to make it into little balls and cook them under the turkey (which is raised on a rack) in the roasting tin. They are usually added to the tin about 1½ hours before the end of cooking time. Alternatively, place the forcemeat in a greased dish, cover with foil and cook in the bottom of the oven for the same length of time as the turkey.

FOR 4.5 KG [10 LB] BIRD
175 g [6 oz] sausage meat
50 g [2 oz] fresh white breadcrumbs
15 ml [1 tablespoon] freshly chopped parsley
1 small onion
1 streaky bacon rasher
1 large egg
salt and black pepper

1 Place the sausage meat in a bowl and stir in the crumbs and parsley.

2 Peel and finely chop the onion and add to the bowl.

3 De-rind the bacon rasher and mince or finely chop it. Add to the bowl. Break the egg into a separate bowl, beat and then stir into the sausage meat mixture so that a smooth paste is formed. Season to taste and use as required.

SPECIAL FORCEMEAT

This is a classic forcemeat which was a favourite of the Edwardians. It is rather expensive for modern tastes but is well worth making if you want to go the whole hog for Christmas dinner. Pounding the meat before adding the other ingredients gives a good contrast of rough and smooth textures.

FOR 4·5 KG [10 LB] BIRD
1 streaky bacon rasher
3 shallots
100 g [¼ lb] pie veal
50 g [2 oz] fresh white breadcrumbs

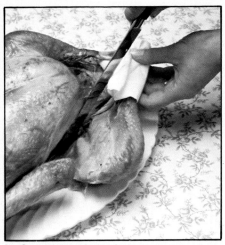

1 Cut through and remove trussing strings. Pull the leg away from the body and cut through the joint where it joins the body.

2 Cut through the centre joint of one leg to divide it into drumsticks and thigh. Slice the meat from the drumstick.

3 To slice thigh, hold firmly on a plate with a fork. Cut slices parallel to the centre bone. Divide other leg in the same way.

---

50 g [2 oz] butter
2 large mushrooms
15 ml [1 tablespoon] freshly
  chopped parsley
salt and black pepper
pinch of cayenne
pinch of mace
1 large egg

1 De-rind the bacon. Skin the shallots. Mince together the veal, bacon and shallots and place in a bowl with the breadcrumbs.

2 Cream the butter until light and fluffy then gradually pound into the mixture a little at a time. An easy way to do this is with either a pestle or the end of a rolling pin.

3 When all the butter has been amalgamated, wipe clean the mushrooms, trim the stalks and chop. Add to the mixture with the parsley and seasonings.

4 Beat the egg in a separate bowl and use to bind the forcemeat.

RAISIN AND NUT STUFFING

This stuffing is quick to make and has a delicious flavour. Salted peanuts give the best taste but you can use any other nuts in their place.

FOR 4·5 KG [10 LB] BIRD
100 g [¼ lb] fresh brown
  breadcrumbs

50 g [2 oz] seedless raisins
50 g [2 oz] salted peanuts
15 ml [1 tablespoon] freshly
  chopped parsley
freshly ground black pepper
1 large egg

1 Place the breadcrumbs in a bowl with the raisins. Roughly chop the nuts and add.

2 Add the parsley. Season to taste with pepper. Beat the egg in a separate bowl and stir into the stuffing mixture to bind it.

CHESTNUT STUFFING

This is the traditional stuffing for turkey. Chestnuts are extremely time consuming to boil and skin so it is quicker and easier to use canned chestnut purée for this dish, especially at the festive season when most cooks have enough to do anyway. Be sure to use the unsweetened variety.

FOR 4·5 KG [10 LB] BIRD
225 g [½ lb] unsweetened
  chestnut purée
1 small onion
25 g [1 oz] fresh white
  breadcrumbs
25 g [1 oz] butter

1 Place the purée in a bowl. Skin and finely chop the onion and add to the purée. Mix well.

2 Stir in the breadcrumbs. Melt the

butter in a heavy-based pan over low heat and add to the dry ingredients. Mix well and leave until cold before use.

STUART STUFFING

The original for this recipe may be found in an anonymous 17th century manuscript in London's Victoria and Albert Museum. It was originally intended for chicken but is very good indeed with turkey, especially when served cold. This stuffing uses the liver from the turkey.

FOR 4·5 KG [10 LB] BIRD
100 g [4 oz] sliced bread
150 ml [¼ pt] milk
1 lemon
15 ml [1 tablespoon] mixed
  finely chopped parsley,
  thyme and chives
1 shallot
15 ml [1 tablespoon] ground
  almonds
salt and black pepper
liver from the turkey

1 Place the bread in a shallow dish. Pour on the milk and leave to soak for 20 minutes.

2 Squash the bread to a pulp with a fork. Grate the zest from the lemon and squeeze the juice. Add the juice and zest to the bread with the herbs.

3 Peel and finely chop the shallot

a large turkey

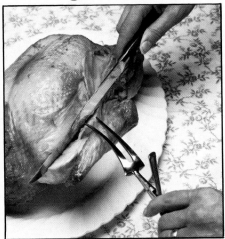

4 To slice the breast, place the knife parallel and as close to the wing as you can. Make a deep cut down the bone.

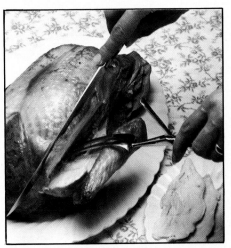

5 Now carve the breast downwards, ending at the deep cut. Do other side in the same way. Remove wings and set aside.

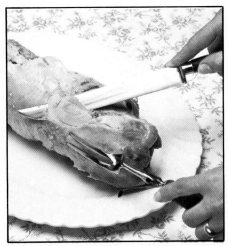

6 Turn the bird over and slice off meat from the base and from the oyster as for chicken.

and add to the mixture with the almonds and seasoning, to taste. Mince the liver and add. Stir well before use.

ROASTING TURKEY

Everyone wants to roast turkey to be a special treat, regardless of the occasion, with crispy golden skin and moist, tender flesh. There are few rules to observe and with a little care you will be guaranteed success every time.

The methods for roasting small and large turkeys vary slightly. All times given here are for stuffed birds. For unstuffed birds, cook for about 5 minutes less per 450 g [1 lb]. When cooking self-basting birds, follow the manufacturer's instructions.

Barding

Both large and small turkeys must be barded to prevent the skin drying out and becoming tough. Do not bard self-basting turkeys as they already have sufficient fat or oil to keep them moist. Either spread the skin of the breast and legs generously with softened or melted butter, and sprinkle with salt to encourage crispness, or lay bacon rashers over the bird. Streaky bacon is best as it has the most fat.

Small birds

Small birds are best cooked at a high heat. This ensures that the flesh is cooked right through but is still moist. This method is suitable for birds weighing up to 3.6 kg [8 lb]. Bard the turkey then place on a piece of foil on a roasting rack in a roasting tin. Roast in the centre of an oven heated to 230°C [450°F] gas mark 8 for 22 minutes per 450 g [1 lb] or until the juices run clear when the flesh is pierced near the thick part of the leg. About 20 minutes before the end of cooking time, open the foil to allow the breast to brown. Baste frequently with the juice in the foil during this time.

When roasting small self-basting birds, follow the manufacturer's instructions.

Large birds

Set the oven to 160°C [325°F] gas mark 3. Bard the bird and then place it on a rack in a large roasting tin in the centre of the oven. Cook, following the times given in the chart. Baste frequently during cooking. Turn the bird every hour to make sure that the skin browns evenly. If the turkey has been barded with bacon rashers, remove these 20 minutes before the end of cooking time. If the breast skin looks as though it will be over browned, cover with a piece of foil. Remove this 5 minutes before the end of cooking time to complete crisping the skin.

If the bird is very large and only just fits into the oven, it may be rather too large for the roasting tin. In this case place the bird on the rack on the centre shelf and the roasting tin on a surface of foil (to catch any stray drips) on the shelf below. Baste with the melted fat caught in the roasting tin.

However large the turkey and long the cooking time, never part-cook the bird the day before. This is a great health hazard as there is a danger that the bird will not be properly heated through and salmonella germs will multiply.

When cooking time is up, test the meat with a skewer in the fleshy part of the leg. If the juices run clear, the bird is cooked. Remove from the oven and leave in a warm place for at least 10 minutes (30 minutes for very large birds) to allow the flesh to set. This makes carving easier.

Turkey rolls

Manufacturers usually recommend that rolls be roasted at 160°C [325°F] gas mark 3 for 15 minutes per 450 g [1 lb]. Always check the label carefully though, as this may vary.

COOKING TIMES FOR LARGE TURKEYS At 160°C [325°C] gas mark 3	
Weight	**Hours**
4–4.5 kg [9–10 lb]	4–4½
4.5–5.5 kg [10–12 lb]	4½–5
5.5–6.8 kg [12–15 lb]	5–5½
6.8–7.7 kg [15–17lb]	5½–6
7.7–9.1 kg [17–20 lb]	6–6½
9.1–11.3 kg [20–25 lb]	6½–7½

CARVING A TURKEY

The three essential requisites for carving a turkey are a sharp knife, a stout carving fork and a spiked carving plate to hold the bird steady while you cut.

Small birds

If you are roasting a small turkey, you will probably want to carve it at the table following the time-honoured family method of a leg or a wing each, and some breast meat.

This is an excellent way to carve a turkey for a small family and is fairly fully understood by every cook. Do remove the stuffing first though—something which is often forgotten when carving by this method.

Large birds

If you have spent a lot of money on a large turkey, you will want it to go as far as possible. This is achieved by clever carving. It is best to carve a large turkey in the kitchen as the process is quite time consuming. As you carve the meat, place it on a warm plate in a warm place then it will not go cold before it gets to the table. When carving turkey in this way, it is customary to give everyone portions made up of some light and some dark meat (ie, breast and leg). Once again, remember to remove the stuffing first and serve it in a separate dish.

COLD TURKEY

If you are roasting turkey to serve cold, it must be cooled as rapidly as possible and then stored, covered, in a refrigerator. When the turkey is cooked, remove from the oven and place on a cold plate. Leave until cool then cover lightly with foil and store in the refrigerator. It will keep for two days. Do not cut the turkey before required or the meat will dry out. To serve left-over turkey hot, it must be completely cooked again—in a stew, curry or casserole, for instance, or brought slowly just up to boiling point in a sauce, to destroy the germs which cause food poisoning. If you have cold sliced turkey left over, wrap it in foil or greaseproof paper and store in the refrigerator.

ACCOMPANIMENTS FOR TURKEY

As befits such a splendid bird, turkey has a wide range of traditional accompaniments.

Chipolata sausages may be cooked in the bottom of the roasting pan and arranged around or at one end of the bird. Be sure to get the real spicy, small chipolatas to serve with turkey.

Forcemeat balls may be made from the forcemeat described in the stuffings section and cooked underneath the turkey. An alternative to making balls is to place the prepared forcemeat in a greased dish, cook in the bottom of the oven for the same time as the turkey but, in the case of a big bird, for no more than 1½ hours. Serve with the bird.

Cranberry sauce has a sharp flavour that contrasts agreeably with the taste and texture of turkey. You can, of course, make your own cranberry sauce if you have the time, but the bottled varieties now on sale are mostly very good.

Bacon rolls are another traditional and tasty accompaniment. Try them stuffed with prunes which have been stoned and soaked overnight in strained cold tea. Drain thoroughly before stuffing.

Bread sauce is to chicken and turkey what mint sauce is to lamb. It's rather strange savoury sweet flavour and creamy texture marries well with both hot and cold turkey. A recipe for a traditional bread sauce is given on page 214.

Gravy for turkey should be thin and brown. For best flavour use giblet stock and follow the recipe given here for turkey gravy.

TURKEY GRAVY

The stock from giblets makes a well-flavoured gravy to accompany turkey. You cannot, however, make a good giblet gravy if the liver is being used for stuffing the bird. If this is the case, use chicken stock to make the gravy instead. Preparation of the giblets must be done carefully otherwise the stock will have a very strong flavour and a cloudy grey appearance. This gravy is traditional but if your family does not like it there is no reason why you should not thicken turkey gravy in the usual way by adding plain flour to the pan juices.

MAKES 250 ML [½ PT]
turkey giblets
half an onion
1 carrot
1 bay leaf
15 ml [1 tablespoon] cranberry jelly

1 Cut away the greenish gall bladder and any green patches on the liver as these will be bitter.

2 Cut up the gizzard as far as the crop. Peel off the flesh and discard the rest.

3 Place the giblets in a pan with the peeled and halved onion, scrubbed and halved carrot, bay leaf and about 250 ml [½ pt] water.

4 Bring gradually to boil and then skim off any scum. Cover and simmer for 2 hours.

5 Strain the stock through a muslin-lined sieve. Leave until cold and then remove any fat which has set on the surface.

6 Bring slowly to the boil while the turkey is roasting.

7 Remove the cooked turkey from the roasting tin and keep in a warm place. Pour the fat away from the tin leaving the sediment behind.

8 Pour the hot giblet stock gradually into the roasting tin, stirring and scraping the bottom of the tin to lift the sediment.

9 When the gravy is a rich brown, set the roasting tin over low heat and bring slowly to the boil.

10 Remove from heat, stir in the cranberry jelly and serve hot.

ROAST TURKEY WITH ORANGE CURRANT STUFFING

⊠⊠⊠ *A small turkey can be made into a family treat if you use an interesting and tasty stuffing. The stuffed apples which accompany this dish make it look especially festive. Red-skinned eating apples look nicest and their flavour contrasts pleasantly with that of the stuffing.*

SERVES 4-6

2.2 kg [5 lb] turkey
100 g [¼ lb] butter
salt
100 g [¼ lb] fresh white
breadcrumbs
75 g [3 oz] shredded suet
1 orange
50 g [2 oz] currants
1 small onion
pinch of nutmeg
freshly ground black pepper
1 medium-sized egg
4 red-skinned eating apples

1 Set the oven to 230°C [450°F] gas mark 8. Grate the zest from the orange and squeeze to extract the juice.

2 Place the breadcrumbs, suet, orange zest and juice and currants in a bowl. Skin and finely chop the onion and add to the bowl.

3 Add the nutmeg and pepper to taste. Break the egg into a separate bowl, beat it and add to the stuffing ingredients.

4 Wash and season the inside of the turkey. Stuff the neck end, leaving 60 ml [4 tablespoons] stuffing for the apples. Truss if necessary.

5 Spread the breast and legs liberally with 50 g [2 oz] butter.

Sprinkle with salt. Wrap in foil.

6 Cook in the centre of the oven for 2 hours. About 25 minutes before the end of cooking time, core the apples and stuff with remaining stuffing. Melt the remaining butter over low heat and brush over the apples. Place the apples in a dish in the oven.

7 About 20 minutes before the end of cooking time, unwrap the turkey to allow the breast to brown.

8 To serve, arrange the stuffed apples around the turkey.

Roast turkey with orange currant stuffing is garnished with baked apples. Cranberry sauce is a traditional accompaniment with roast turkey.

SPICY ROAST TURKEY

◪◪ *Rubbing the skin of turkey with spiced butter gives an unusual flavour which contrasts pleasantly with the bacon and olive stuffing. If you wish, soaked prunes may be substituted for stuffed olives as they go equally well with bacon.*

SERVES 4
2.2 kg [5 lb] turkey
salt
freshly ground black pepper
25 g [1 oz] white breadcrumbs
50 g [2 oz] streaky bacon
25 g [1 oz] stuffed green olives
25 g [1 oz] walnuts
3 garlic cloves
1 small egg
50 g [2 oz] butter
5 ml [1 teaspoon] ground cinnamon
2.5 ml [½ teaspoon] ground cloves

1 Wash the turkey and season inside with salt and freshly ground black pepper.

2 Set the oven to 230°C [450°F] gas mark 8.

3 Place the breadcrumbs in a bowl. De-rind the bacon, cut into small pieces and add to the bowl. Chop the olives and walnuts and add to the bowl.

4 Skin and chop the garlic cloves and add to the bowl. Beat the egg in a separate bowl and stir into the mixture.

5 Stuff the neck of the turkey with the mixture and then truss if necessary.

6 Beat the butter in a bowl until soft and creamy. Mix in 5 ml [1 teaspoon] freshly ground black pepper, the cinnamon, the cloves and a pinch of salt.

7 Spread the turkey breast and legs liberally with the spiced butter. Wrap in foil.

8 Cook in the centre of the oven on a rack for 2 hours. About 20 minutes before the end of cooking time, unwrap the foil to brown the breast. Baste frequently with the juices during this time. When cooked transfer to a serving plate to rest before carving.

BUFFET TURKEY WITH CAMBRIDGE SAUCE

◪◪ *If you have a large number of people to feed, a turkey roll is the perfect choice. Turkey rolls are easy to carve and economical because there is no waste. Turkey meat served alone can, however, be rather uninteresting, so choose a sharp sauce to offset the blandness of the meat. Cambridge sauce, a favourite of 19th century dons and deans fits the bill perfectly. Its pale colour blends well with the meat.*

SERVES 12
1.4 kg [3 lb] turkey roll
50 g [2 oz] softened butter
salt

For the sauce:
4 medium-sized hard-boiled eggs
50 g [2 oz] anchovy fillets
15 ml [1 tablespoon] capers
15 ml [1 tablespoon] freshly chopped chives
15 ml [1 tablespoon] freshly chopped tarragon
10 ml [2 teaspoons] French mustard
30 ml [2 tablespoons] red wine vinegar
90 ml [6 tablespoons] olive oil
15 ml [1 tablespoon] freshly chopped parsley
2.5 ml [½ teaspoon] cayenne pepper

Buffet turkey with Cambridge sauce.

1 Set the oven to 160°C [325°F], gas mark 3. Spread butter over the turkey roll and sprinkle with salt.

2 Place the turkey roll on a rack in a roasting tin. Place in the centre of the oven and cook for 1¼ hours, basting from time to time.

3 Remove the turkey roll from the oven. Allow to become cold before slicing.

4 Meanwhile, make the sauce. Cut the hard-boiled eggs in half and remove the yolks.

5 Place yolks in a mortar with the anchovies, capers, tarragon, chives and mustard. Pound with a pestle until you have a smooth cream. Alternatively, place the ingredients in a bowl and pound with the end of a rolling pin.

6 Stir the vinegar into the mixture. Now add the oil a drop at a time as for mayonnaise until the sauce turns thick.

7 When the sauce is thick, strain. Add the parsley and cayenne pepper.

8 Slice the cold turkey thinly and serve with the sauce.

Out for a duck!

Roasted correctly, duck and goose are delicious. Roasted badly, they are positively unpleasant. Duck is more readily available today than ever before while goose, pushed out of its traditional role as the Christmas bird by the turkey, deserves a come-back. Here you will see how to roast both birds to perfection, and how to make a number of classic dishes.

Duck is prized for its pronounced flavour and succulence. Unfortunately, it is not a very fleshy bird and consequently the meat does not go very far. Nor are the birds very large. You will never be able to feed more than four people from a single duck.

Geese are larger but, again, are not fleshy. When roasted, a goose will feed a maximum of eight people.

When it is to be roasted, the bird should always be young and tender. Strictly speaking, a duck which is less than three months old is correctly called a duckling but the terms duck and duckling are used fairly loosely. A young goose is called a gosling but older birds (up to about a year) are also suitable for roasting.

CHOOSING DOMESTIC DUCKS

Domestic ducks come prepared in four different ways — New York dressed, fresh oven-ready, chilled and frozen. A guide which applies to all, is to choose a bird weighing between 1.4–2.2 kg [3–5 lb]. Birds of this weight are still young and tender.

Duck has a distinctive flavour and its flesh is dark and rather rich. Fresh fruit complements the flavour particularly well.

Remember that frozen birds take up water and thus weight, during the freezing process, and that the weight of a New York dressed bird is increased by about a third by the head, feet and innards. When choosing any kind of duck, look for a plump breast and creamy white skin. The legs should be well rounded.

New York dressed
New York dressed birds are seen

hanging in butchers' shops, with head and feet attached. If the bill and feet are pale yellow and the bill is flexible, you will know you are buying a young bird. Like all New York dressed birds, ducks prepared in this way are quite expensive per 450 g [1 lb] because you are paying for the head, feet and innards. These can add up to one third on the weight. Flavour is not really that much better than chilled oven-ready birds, so the expense of a New York dressed bird is not really justified.

Fresh oven-ready

These are birds which have been completely prepared for the oven. Giblets are usually sold with the bird. They are slightly less expensive than New York dressed and a good buy if you are adamant about having fresh duck.

Chilled

Chilled birds are sold pre-packed and oven-ready. They are cheaper than fresh birds and a good buy because there is no uptake of water as with frozen birds.

Frozen

The large scale production and freezing of duck has been responsible for a greater interest in the bird. Frozen ducks are sold completely oven-ready. All you have to do is thaw the bird thoroughly. Some weight is lost when the duck is thawed because it will lose the water taken in during the freezing process. Frozen ducks are the cheapest and are an excellent buy if you plan to roast with a well-flavoured stuffing.

Also available are frozen duck portions. These are made up of leg and breast and are a good buy for a dinner à deux as they cut down on preparation and carving.

CHOOSING WILD DUCKS

Wild ducks are only available fresh and are limited by the game seasons. The main varieties of wild duck sold for eating in the United Kingdom are teal, widgeon and mallard. They are in season from late August to March. Wild ducks are small. Widgeon are the largest but rarely come in weights greater than 1.6 kg [3½ lb].

Wild ducks are almost always sold New York dressed or feathered: an expensive buy, as a lot of weight is lost once the inedible parts have

been removed.

If a sporting member of your family goes shooting and bags a duck, hang it head down for three days before plucking and drawing.

There is very little to choose between teal, mallard and widgeon. They all have rather coarse, strongly flavoured flesh. Usually you have to take pot luck on what is available when buying.

CHOOSING DOMESTIC GEESE

Because geese are temperamental birds (so fierce are they that Scottish distilleries use them instead of dogs to guard the whisky), they cannot be intensively reared. This means they are still farmed in a small way, so are always expensive. Consequently, the supply of domestic geese follows their natural life cycle and they are only readily available towards the close of the year.

The season for geese begins in late September with the traditional Michaelmas goose that was given as a tithe for hundreds of years. The season ends in March with the so-called green geese or goslings of Easter.

Geese are sold either New York dressed or oven-ready. As already explained, New York dressed means expensive. Up to half the weight of a goose can be lost once the head, feet and entrails are removed. Oven-ready birds are always sold fresh and work out to be marginally cheaper. It is not advisable to buy a goose over 4.5 kg [10 lb] as the flesh of an older bird can be very stringy. Nor is it advisable to buy a goose under 2.7 kg [6 lb] as you will be paying for more bone than flesh.

Wild geese

Wild geese are rarely sold commercially. They have a strong, gamey flavour and are inclined to be very stringy. Should a member of your family shoot one, casserole it or use it for pâté. Roast wild goose is not recommended.

HOW MUCH TO BUY

One of the sad things about duck and goose is that neither bird goes very far. They both have a very high proportion of bone to flesh and this means you have to allow quite a lot of bird per person to get a reasonable

portion. However, the bones make a very good gamey stock which can be used for soups and the fat is exceptionally flavoursome and is excellent for frying meat or sautéing or roasting potatoes.

Domestic duck is the fleshiest of the birds discussed but even so you will need to allow a minimum of 450 g [1 lb] oven-ready weight per person. In practice, allow a bit over so if you are serving four, count on a 2.2 kg [5 lb] bird (oven-ready weight), to allow good-sized portions.

Wild ducks are small and also bony. When buying teal, allow one plump bird (about 700 g [1½ lb] per person). When buying widgeon and mallard, allow at least 450 g [1 lb] per person, as for domestic duck.

Geese are even bonier than ducks. When buying a goose, you must allow 700 g [1½ lb] of dressed bird per person.

PREPARING FOR ROASTING

Duck and goose are prepared for roasting in similar ways. The main difference is the trussing and the removal of fat from inside a goose.

Duck

First thaw the bird thoroughly if frozen. Thaw it in the bag and allow 1½ hours per 450 g [1 lb] at room temperature or 2½ hours per 450 g [1 lb] in the refrigerator.

Cleaning: remove the giblets if inside and rinse the bird under cold water inside and out. Pat dry carefully, both inside and out, and season the inside with salt and pepper.

Stuffing: domestic ducks are stuffed through the tail end, not the neck. A sharp, tangy stuffing is almost essential to contrast with the rich flesh. A suitable stuffing for duck is sage and onion. Also good are those given in the recipe section here. Allow 25 g [1 oz] stuffing per 450 g [1 lb] of duck. Do not stuff the duck until just before you roast it and do not make the stuffing in advance. Stuffing is such a mixture of ingredients that it can easily spoil and may even become a health hazard.

Trussing: after stuffing, ducks are trussed with string in exactly the same way as a chicken except that the wings are not pinned to the back. Trussing a chicken is discussed in detail on pages 16–17.

The skin: domestic duck has a thick

Handy hints

In the North of England, one of the more bizarre uses of goose fat was to spread it on the chest of anyone suffering from a cold and then wrap them up in a brown paper waistcoat. The unfortunate sufferer was then sent to bed with a hot water bottle and supposedly awoke cured, after a smelly night!

● The fat from duck and goose is exceptionally well flavoured and should be saved for use in fry-start casseroles, for sealing meat, for roasting and for making pâtés. It also makes delicious fried bread and sautéed potatoes.

● When you render down the solid fat from inside a goose, you will find little crisp pieces are left behind. These are called frittons d'oie. If you pound them to make a paste, they are a delicious spread for toast.

● Store your goose or duck fat in a jar in the refrigerator or freezer. Covered with cling film it will last for three months.

layer of fat under the skin so there is no need to bard the bird. Prick the skin lightly all over with a fork. This will encourage the fat to flow out during cooking. Then rub the skin generously with salt and freshly ground black pepper. This will give a lovely flavour and also help to crisp the skin.

Wild ducks are cleaned, then seasoned inside and trussed but not stuffed as they are too small for this. Prick the thighs to allow excess fat to run out and rub the skin with salt and pepper. The breast of wild duck is much drier than that of domestic duck, so it must be barded with strips of streaky bacon. The bacon is laid across the breast and is removed about 20 minutes before the end of cooking to allow the breast to brown and crisp.

Goose

A goose is cleaned and seasoned in the same way as a duck.

Removing fat: inside a goose, underneath and around the flap of skin at the neck end, there is a large amount of solid white fat. This must be removed before the goose is roasted or it would be impossibly greasy. To remove the fat, simply pull it away with your hands. Render the fat down and use it in the ways suggested.

Stuffing: like duck, goose needs a sharp stuffing to contrast with the rich flesh. When stuffing a goose, you will need 40 g [1½ oz] stuffing for every 450 g [1 lb] goose, dressed weight. Goose is, like duck, stuffed through the tail end.

Trussing: a goose is trussed with skewers rather than with string. You will need three long, plain metal skewers. First, press the wings close to the sides of the bird. Pass a skewer through the centre joint and out at the other side. Pass another skewer through the wing tips. Push the legs

Duck, roasted and served with some simply cooked fresh vegetables, makes a pleasant change from the usual Sunday joint.

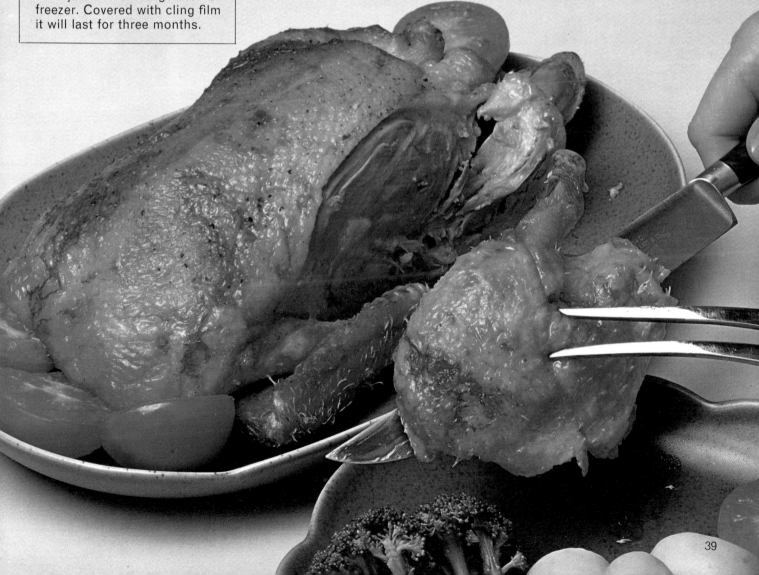

1 Prepare the required quantity of stuffing for the bird. Heat the oven to 220°C [425°F] gas mark 7.

2 Rinse bird and pat dry. Remove solid fat from inside goose. Season inside the bird.

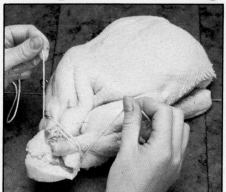

3 Stuff through the tail end. Truss a duck with string in the same way as a chicken.

7 Place the bird on a rack in a roasting tin. Roast for 15 minutes. Reduce heat as specified in text.

8 Roast for 18 minutes per 450 g [1 lb]. Pour off excess fat from tin at regular intervals.

9 Turn the tin from time to time so that the bird browns evenly on all sides.

close to the sides of the bird. Push a skewer through the thickest part of the leg and right through the bird.
The skin: the skin of a goose is prepared in exactly the same way as domestic duck.

ROASTING
Duck and goose are roasted in the same way. Wild duck is roasted in a slightly different way which is given in a separate section.

Domestic duck and goose
Place the prepared bird on its back on a rack in a roasting tin. The rack prevents the bird from sitting in a pool of grease while in the oven. Set the oven to 220°C [425°F] gas mark 7 and when the temperature has been reached, place the roasting tin on the centre shelf. Cook for fifteen minutes at this temperature. This initial period at high temperature starts the fat flowing. After fifteen minutes reduce the heat to 180°C [350°F] gas

mark 4 for duck, 190°C [375°F] gas mark 5 for goose and roast for eighteen minutes per 450 g [1 lb].

During roasting, do not baste the bird at all but tip the excess fat out of the tin every fifteen minutes or so. Hold the bird securely in place by the legs, or remove it from the tin. The fat from the body cavity of a goose can be poured out into the tin by tilting the bird on to its tail end with a fish slice. Place a gloved hand on the body of the goose to prevent it slipping. Then tip the fat from the tin, holding the bird in place. If the goose is stuffed, it will not be possible to tip the cavity fat out at the tail end. The fat will remain in the cavity and some of it be absorbed by the stuffing. Turn the tin several times during roasting so that the bird browns evenly.

Twenty minutes before the end of roasting, turn the bird upside down to brown its back. Turn it breast side up again 5 minutes before the end of roasting, to give the breast skin a final crisping. The bird is cooked when the

juices run clear. To test this, pierce at the thick part of the leg with a skewer.

Wild duck
Because it is less fatty, the breast of wild duck is barded with bacon before roasting. The duck is then roasted at a constant temperature of 220°C [425°F] gas mark 7 for 10 minutes per 450 g [1 lb]. Half way through cooking, remove the bacon barding strips and pour 45 ml [3 tablespoons] port or fresh orange juice over the bird. Baste frequently, every five minutes or so after this. Teal is quickest to cook being smallest. An average teal will cook in twenty minutes. Mallard and widgeon take about 30 minutes.

CARVING DUCK AND GOOSE
Ducks and geese are rather an odd shape and because of this are not easy to carve. It is simpler, by far, to portion a duck, either in two or in

domestic duck and goose

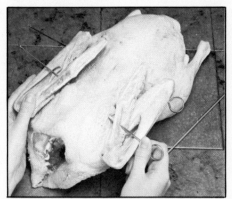

4 Truss a goose with skewers. Push one through the centre joint and one through the wing tip.

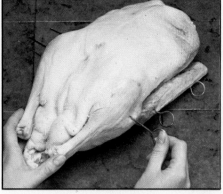

5 Turn the bird on to its back and press the legs to the body. Push the skewer through the thighs.

6 Prick the skin all over to allow fat to escape and rub with salt and freshly ground black pepper.

10 About 20 minutes before the end of roasting, turn bird upside down to brown the back.

11 Turn breast side up 5 minutes before the end of roasting for a final browning and crisping.

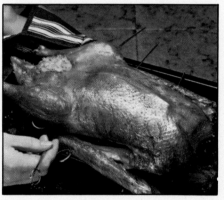

12 To test if cooked, pierce the thick part of the leg with a skewer. The juices should run clear.

four. However, a large duck can be carved in the same way as a goose. Either job is better completed in the kitchen, whenever possible. Carving takes some time and when done in the kitchen, the carved meat can be kept hot. Wild duck, which is served one per person, obviously needs no carving or portioning.

Portioning a duck

To portion a duck, place the bird on a board and remove the trussing strings. If stuffed, remove the stuffing and serve separately. Sit the bird upright and, with a very sharp knife, cut down through the breast-bone and through the backbone and right along the length of the duck. This gives you two portions. Lay each half flat and make a slanting cut upwards over the leg to separate the leg and wing. Any rib bones sticking out can be snipped off with kitchen scissors. You now have four portions of approximately equal weight, each with some breast meat.

Carving a goose or duck

To carve a goose or duck, first remove the trussing and leave the bird to rest in a warm place for about fifteen minutes for the flesh to set. (This also gives you time to make the gravy.) A spiked carving plate will hold the bird steady and make carving much easier.

If the bird is stuffed, first remove the stuffing before you start carving and serve separately. This is best done with a spoon so that you can spoon out the surplus from inside the body cavity.

Begin carving by removing the legs. These are set differently to those of a chicken and join the body under the bird's back. Cut through at the joint and remove. Do not carve the meat from the legs but sever the thigh from the drumstick. Cut off the wings, slicing off a piece of breast with each.

To carve the breast, make the first cut along the breastbone, right down to the carcass. Carve the meat in thick

slices working down each side of the breast, cutting into the bird. The slices will still be attached to the bird at this point. Loosen the slices by cutting upwards, with the knife held flat against the carcass. You will then have long, narrow slices of breast meat.

To serve, lay the breast slices in the centre of the serving platter, place the legs at one end, wings at the other, and pour over a little gravy. Garnish with suitable vegetables, fruit or greenery.

ACCOMPANIMENTS FOR DUCK AND GOOSE

Duck and goose have similar accompaniments.

Giblet gravy

Make giblet gravy in the same way as for chicken on page 210. The addition of 45 ml (3 tablespoons) port or orange juice goes very well with both duck and goose. A little red-

Step-by-step to carving a goose

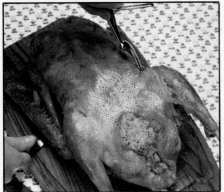

1 Remove trussing and leave bird to rest for 15 minutes. Place it on a spiked carving plate.

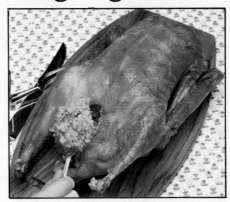

2 Remove the stuffing with a spoon before starting to carve. Keep hot while carving.

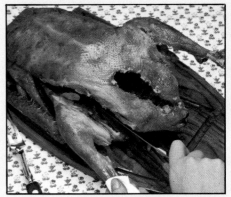

3 Ease each leg away from the body. Cut through at joint with body, under the back. Separate thigh.

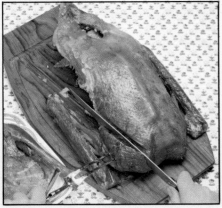

4 Ease each wing away from the body and cut off, slicing off some breast meat with each wing.

5 Cut down along the breastbone. Carve breast by cutting into the bird, parallel to the first cut.

6 Loosen the slices by cutting upwards, holding the knife flat against the body of the bird.

currant jelly stirred into the gravy also gives good flavour. If you can get them, crab apples sliced into rings and cooked in the pan below the duck or goose give the gravy a good flavour. If you cannot get crab apples, cooking apples may be used instead.

Other accompaniments

Redcurrant jelly offsets the rich flavour of duck and goose. Ready-made redcurrant jelly is widely available and perfectly presentable.

Sliced oranges and bunches of watercress make an attractive garnish which complements the flavour of duck and goose.

Vegetables to accompany duck and goose should always be very plain as the main interest of the meal lies in the meat. Julienne potatoes (strips) or game chips (crisps), grilled tomatoes, green peas or beans or boiled new potatoes are all suitable.

Stuffings should be slightly sharp and fruit is often included.

Fruit accompaniments are particularly good with plainly roasted duck or goose—try the stuffed spiced peaches given here.

Apple rings fried in butter are a traditional accompaniment for both duck and goose. To make, peel, core and slice the dessert apples. Fry lightly in butter until just browned.

Baked oranges are seldom seen today but they too deserve a revival for plainly cooked duck or goose. They are also good with pork.

BAKED ORANGES

Baked oranges are an old-fashioned accompaniment for duck, goose or pork and are cooked in the oven at the same time. Choose medium-sized oranges with brightly coloured skins. This usually indicates that they are juicy.

If being baked alone, the oven temperature required is 180°C [350°F] gas mark 4.

SERVES 4

4 medium-sized oranges
20 ml [4 teaspoons] brown sugar
50 g [2 oz] unsalted butter
20 ml [4 teaspoons] sweet sherry

1 Cut a thin slice off the top of each orange. Using a grapefruit knife, cut around inside the orange from the top, to loosen the flesh.

2 Remove the flesh from the skin shell. Holding the flesh over a plate to catch the juice, divide into segments, discarding membrane, pith and pips.

3 Return the segments of orange and juice to the shell. Place 5 ml [1 teaspoon] sugar in each shell. Divide the butter into four and place a piece in each shell.

4 Place the oranges in a dish. Pour

in enough hot water to come half way up the oranges. This prevents the skins drying out. Bake for 30 minutes on the floor of the oven while you are cooking your bird.

5 Just before serving, pour 5 ml [1 teaspoon] sherry into each orange.

SPICED PEACHES

Stuffed, spiced peaches are simplicity itself to make. Choose firm rather than very ripe peaches. Very ripe fruit may well disintegrate. The peaches are cooked in the oven at the same time as the meat. Spiced peaches can also be cooked under a moderate grill for 3–4 minutes until golden.

SERVES 4
4 medium-sized peaches
45 ml [3 tablespoons] brown sugar
50 g [2 oz] butter
pinch of ground nutmeg
pinch of ground cloves
45 ml [3 tablespoons] orange juice (optional)

1 Skin, halve and stone the peaches.

2 Mix together the sugar, butter and spices. Use about half of the mixture to fill the stone cavities in the peaches.

3 Place the peaches in a shallow baking dish. Dot the rest of the butter and spice mixture around them. Add 45 ml [3 tablespoons] of orange juice or water.

4 Bake on the floor of the oven while you are roasting your duck or goose, for 30 minutes. Spoon the juices over the peaches from time to time.

STUFFINGS

All the stuffings given here are for a 3.6 kg [8 lb] goose or for a 2.2 kg [5 lb] duck. Remember that you need 40 g [1½ oz] stuffing per 450 g [1 lb] goose and 25 g [1 oz] per 450 g [1 lb] duck. All stuffings should be cool before being put into the bird.

APPLE AND POTATO STUFFING

This rather filling stuffing is used mostly to extend goose which does

not go very far. If you can get them, crab apples have a sharper flavour and give the best results. For convenience the potatoes can be made in advance and allowed to cool. For this recipe there is no need to include an egg.

STUFFS 1 GOOSE
100 g [¼ lb] creamed potatoes
100 g [¼ lb] onions
2 sprigs lemon thyme
2 sprigs savory or parsley
1 orange
100 g [¼ lb] crab or cooking apples

1 Place the creamed potatoes (either freshly made or ready cooked) in a bowl.

2 Skin and finely chop the onions and add to the potatoes.

3 Chop the herbs and add. Grate the zest from the orange and add to the bowl. Squeeze, and add the

juice to the other ingredients.

4 Peel and chop the apples. Add to the stuffing. Leave to cool if necessary.

ORANGE STUFFING FOR DUCK

Duck and oranges are a well-known combination. This stuffing could be used for goose, in which case increase the quantity by half.

STUFFS 1 DUCK
2 medium-sized onions
2 celery sticks
50 g [2 oz] butter
50 g [2 oz] fresh brown breadcrumbs
2 lemons
3 oranges
pinch of mace
salt
freshly ground black pepper
1 large egg

Step-by-step to portioning a duck

1 Place the bird on a board and remove the trussing strings. Spoon out stuffing, if stuffed.

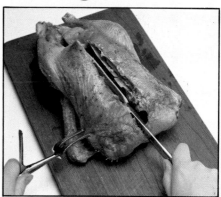

2 Sit the bird on its back. Cut down along the breastbone and through the backbone to halve the duck.

3 Lay each half flat on the board. Make a slanting cut, up over the leg, to separate leg from wing.

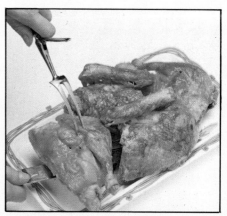

4 Tidy up any jagged bones with kitchen scissors. This gives you four portions, all with breast.

43

1 Skin and finely chop the onions. Scrub and chop the celery.

2 Melt the butter in a heavy-based pan over low heat. Add the onions and celery and cook for 2 minutes so that they are coated in butter but not coloured.

3 Transfer to a bowl and add the breadcrumbs. Grate the zest from the lemons and squeeze them to extract the juice. Add the zest and juice to the bowl.

4 Grate the zest and extract the juice from 1 orange. Add to the bowl.

5 Skin and divide the other oranges into segments. Chop the flesh and add to the bowl.

6 Add the spice and seasonings of salt and pepper.

7 Beat the egg separately and then mix in to bind the stuffing.

APPLE AND PRUNE STUFFING

◪ *This is the most famous of all the stuffings for goose. It can be used for duck as well, in which case reduce the quantity by about a third. For extra flavour, soak the prunes overnight in cold tea to which you have added a piece of cinnamon stick.*

STUFFS 1 GOOSE
75 g [3 oz] fresh brown breadcrumbs
12 prunes, soaked
1 apple
25 g [1 oz] chopped hazelnuts
salt
freshly ground black pepper
1 lemon
15 ml [1 tablespoon] butter
1 large egg

1 Place the breadcrumbs in a bowl. Stone and chop the prunes and add to the bowl.

2 Peel, core and chop the apple. Add to the bowl with the nuts.

3 Season to taste. Squeeze the lemon and add the lemon juice.

4 Melt the butter over low heat and add to the mixture. Beat the egg separately and then use to bind the stuffing.

GOOSE WITH GARLIC STUFFING

◪◪◪ *This recipe comes from the Auvergne, an area famous for both its geese and its garlic. Although the quantity of garlic used looks frighteningly large, the resulting dish carries only a delicate aroma. In the Auvergne, geese are fed on a diet of chestnuts and fine wheat so they are plump and delicious. The goose should be taken to the table flaming and carved at the table.*

SERVES 6
3.6 kg [8 lb] oven-ready goose
100 g [¼ lb] fresh brown breadcrumbs
12 stuffed green olives
1 cooking apple
24 garlic cloves
1 onion
1 lemon
1 medium-sized egg
60 ml [4 tablespoons] calvados

1 Clean the goose and prepare for stuffing as described. Set the oven to 220°C [425°F] gas mark 7.

2 Place the breadcrumbs in a bowl. Chop the olives and peel, core and chop the apple. Peel and chop the garlic cloves and the onion and add all these to the bowl.

3 Grate the zest from the lemon and squeeze to extract the juice. Add the lemon juice and zest to the bowl together with the egg. Mix well to bind.

4 Stuff the goose and complete preparation for roasting.

5 Roast the goose as described in the step-by-step instructions.

6 At the end of cooking, remove the goose to a serving dish. Warm the calvados in a ladle and pour over the breast of the goose. Flambé and take the goose to the table while the flames are still burning.

ROAST GOOSE WITH BEER AND CRANBERRY SAUCE

◪◪◪ *This is an old British recipe, traditionally served at Michaelmas when geese were given to landlords and squires as a tithe from tenants. Brown ale is best but if you cannot obtain this, use stout. Make stock with the giblets in advance.*

SERVES 6
3.6 kg [8 lb] oven-ready goose
salt
freshly ground black pepper

For the stuffing:
100 g [¼ lb] fresh white breadcrumbs
150 ml [¼ pt] milk
2 celery sticks
50 g [2 oz] sultanas
50 g [2 oz] goose liver
1 small onion
15 ml [1 tablespoon] freshly chopped sage

For the sauce:
225 g [½ lb] cooking or crab apples
1 medium-sized onion
100 g [¼ lb] cranberries
150 ml [¼ pt] brown ale or stout
30 ml [2 tablespoons] brown sugar
5 ml [1 teaspoon] vinegar
30 ml [2 tablespoons] fresh brown breadcrumbs
pinch of dry English mustard
pinch of cinnamon

1 Prepare the goose for stuffing and set the oven to 220°C [425°F] gas mark 7.

2 Soak the white breadcrumbs in the milk for 15 minutes. Scrub and chop the celery sticks and add them together with the sultanas.

3 Mince and add the goose liver. Skin and chop the onion and add. Add the sage and season to taste.

4 Stuff the goose and complete preparation for roasting. Roast as described in the step-by-step instructions.

5 Meanwhile, prepare the sauce. Peel, core and chop the cooking apples or peel and core the crab apples. Skin and chop the onion and simmer with the apples and cranberries in the beer for 30 minutes until tender. Add the remaining ingredients, simmer for a further five minutes and set aside to keep warm.

6 When the goose is cooked remove the trussing and leave it in a warm place to rest. Make a giblet gravy in the same way as given for turkey on page 34.

The combination of goose, cranberries and beer produces a full-flavoured dish.

7 Carve the goose and arrange the meat on a warmed serving platter. Serve sauce and gravy separately.

ROAST DUCK WITH NUT SAUCE

Although this list of ingredients looks rather forbidding, this is not a time-consuming dish to make. Make the giblet stock before starting on the bird itself.

SERVES 4
2.2 kg [5 lb] oven-ready duck
salt
freshly ground black pepper

For the stuffing:
50 g [2 oz] fresh brown breadcrumbs
1 celery stick
1 small onion
1 orange
1 lemon
1 small egg

For the sauce:
250 ml [½ pt] duck giblet stock
2 shallots
100 g [¼ lb] walnut halves
5 ml [1 teaspoon] plain flour
half a lemon
150 ml [¼ pt] sweet sherry

2 dessert apples
1 bunch watercress
15 ml [1 tablespoon] freshly chopped parsley

1 Prepare the duck for roasting but do not truss. Heat the oven to 220°C [425°F] gas mark 7.

2 Place the breadcrumbs in a bowl. Scrub and chop the celery stick and skin and chop the onion and add. Grate the zest from the orange and lemon and squeeze the juice. Add the citrus zest and juice to the bowl. Crack the egg into the bowl and bind the mixture. Stuff the duck and complete preparation for roasting, as described.

3 Roast the duck, following the step-by-step instructions. Reserve any excess fat which is poured off.

4 When the duck is cooked, remove it to a serving platter and keep warm. Pour off the fat from the roasting tin and reserve. Add half the stock to the remaining pan juices.

5 Place 45 ml [3 tablespoons] of the reserved duck fat in a heavy-based pan. Skin and chop the shallots and add to the pan with the walnuts. Cook for 1 minute over medium heat then remove from heat and stir in the flour. Return to heat and cook for 1 minute.

6 Remove from heat again and add the remaining duck stock gradually. Return to heat and simmer for 5 minutes to thicken, stirring all the time.

7 Squeeze the juice from the half lemon. Add the sherry and lemon juice to the sauce. Pour the sauce into the roasting tin, mix with the stock and juices and simmer over low heat for 5 minutes, scraping the sediment from the bottom. Keep warm over very low heat.

8 Peel, core and slice the apples into rings. Fry for 2 minutes on each side in the remaining reserved duck fat.

9 Portion the duck and garnish with the parsley, apple rings and watercress sprigs. Spoon a little of the sauce over the apple rings and serve the rest separately.

Three braces of freshly killed game birds. On the left are a hen and a cock pheasant, on the right a hen and a cock capercaillie and below these a plover and grouse.

Gamesmanship

Game birds, beautiful creatures both to look at and to eat, have a unique flavour. They are, however, not easily obtainable and are only available to cooks for a short period of the year. From the wild moors of Scotland and the peaceful lowlands of England come some of the world's best game birds, so roast game birds, described in detail here, may be considered something of a British speciality.

Game is the general term for any edible wild bird or animal which can be hunted. In the United Kingdom and many other countries most birds (with the exception of wood-pigeon and guinea fowl) are protected by law during certain times of the year so that they may breed. In the close season, as it is called, game birds may not be shot so you will never see them in a butcher's or poulterer's. As most birds come, like Christmas, but once a year, it is well worth sampling their unique flavour while the opportunity exists.

Game birds breed in the cool temperate areas of the northern hemisphere (and occasionally warmer temperate areas too), and a large selection is found in Britain. Traditionally, game birds lived a free and natural life on moorland, heath and pasture and dodged death when the sportsmen and their guns were in hot pursuit. Today, however, the rearing and shooting of game tends to be a much more controlled affair. This has become necessary in order to protect the species. Birds are now killed only under license at certain times of the year and are being bred on farms and in special hatcheries to be released during the season to keep shoots well stocked for the clients, who come from all over the world for the chance of taking a pot shot at a British game bird. Some game birds (quail and guinea fowl for instance) live all their lives on game farms and are killed in exactly the same way as chickens or other domestic fowl.

With the exception of wild ducks (see on page 38), British game birds come from the pheasant, partridge, grouse and wader families. Many are small birds and will serve one or at most two people. This means that game birds are not exactly family fare but they do come into their own when something special is required for an intimate dinner party for perhaps four people, or for a romantic dinner for two. Although game birds are often thought of as very expensive, they are much cheaper than other luxury meats such as steak or the better cuts of veal—a good point to bear in mind when you want to put on the style without breaking the bank.

CHOOSING GAME BIRDS
The most important thing when choosing game for roasting is determining its age. With youth, comes tenderness: with age and extensive dashing around the countryside comes stringiness.

Determining age is easy when the bird is feathered, much harder when it is plucked, so for this reason it is better to buy feathered rather than oven-ready game.

Hanging is also very important as this develops the flavour of the bird. Most good poulterers (the best person to buy from) sell birds which have been hung for the correct length of time or, if you order in advance, the poulterer will hang a bird for you and prepare it for roasting.

Weight
Knowing how much to buy when you choose the bird feathered can be difficult as game birds have lush plumage which can hide a puny body. For this reason, it is wise to deduct 50 per cent from the weight of a large bird, 35 per cent from the weight of a smaller bird. Some game birds are not drawn before roasting. The list overleaf tells you which these are, and how many people each bird will serve. Generally speaking, you should allow 350–450 g [¾–1 lb] oven-ready bird per person.

SEASONS FOR BRITISH GAME BIRDS

Black grouse	August 20th–December 20th (September 1st–December 20th in Somerset, Devon and the New Forest)
Capercaillie	As black grouse
Guinea fowl	All the year round
Partridge	September 1st–February 1st
Pheasant	October 1st–January 31st (England) October 1st–December 10th (Scotland)
Pigeon	All the year round
Plover	August 20th–December 10th
Ptarmigan	August 20th–December 10th
Quail	All the year round
Red grouse	August 12th–December 10th
Snipe	August 12th–December 20th
Woodcock	October 1st–December 20th

Grouse

Perhaps the best known of all game birds, red grouse has a subtle yet distinctive flavour of the Scottish heather on which it feeds. Red grouse is indigenous to the British Isles and has defied all attempts to transplant it elsewhere in the world.

The best Scottish grouse, perfect for roasting, are those shot in the same year in which they hatched. These young birds can be distinguished by their pointed flight feathers and soft down under the wings. The female has brownish plumage with dark bars, the male a dark back and a white breast. Both have little 'trousers' of white feathers down their legs. There is very little difference in flavour between the male and the female bird though the female tends to be a bit plumper. If you buy a brace, you will get one of each.

If the grouse is very small, allow one each. If larger, allow one between two. Grouse should be hung for seven days in summer, nine days in winter or in frosty weather.

Black grouse

The black grouse, sometimes called black cock or black game, is slightly larger than the red grouse but similar in flavour. The male is black with a lyre-shaped tail. The female is smaller than the male and is brown with darker bars. Not often seen in butchers and poulterers but the same rules as red grouse apply when choosing. Hang it for the same length of time as red grouse.

Capercaillie

Also called the cock o' the wood or wood grouse, this is the largest British grouse and has been mistaken for an airborne turkey! The male is dark grey with a long, broad tail. The female is similar to the female black grouse but is slightly larger and has a chestnut patch on its breast. Choose your birds as for red grouse. A male bird will serve two, a female one. Hang your birds as for red grouse.

Ptarmigan

Yet another member of the grouse family, the ptarmigan is rarely seen in poulterers. In winter, both male and female are all white. In summer, the upper parts are a greyish buff. Choose your birds as for grouse. A ptarmigan will serve one. Hang your birds as for red grouse.

Partridge

Partridge is the perfect introduction to eating game, as it has a more delicate flavour than many other birds. The flavour of a young partridge, fattened on stubble where they habitually feed, is not unlike that of a very superior chicken.

Both male and female birds have a greyish breast, barred wings and a chestnut coloured face. A young partridge will have pale yellow feet and fluffy down under the wings. The French draw a useful distinction between old and young partridges. The young partridge they call a perdreau, the older one a perdrix.

Perdreau become perdrix on 1st October and about three weeks after this date are better left for casseroling. A partridge will serve 1-2, depending on size. Partridge should be hung for only 3 days as prolonged hanging spoils the delicate flavour.

Pheasant

Pheasants are the most handsome of the larger game birds. The hen is small with muted brown plumage, the cock is larger with brilliant russet feathers, a long sweeping tail and a beautiful bright green head. Like partridge, pheasants feed on stubble fields and have a similar though rather stronger flavour.

A young cock pheasant will have short, rounded spurs on the legs. The flight feathers should be rounded and downy underneath. The hen is a small, plump bird. A young hen has pale feet and pale plumage. Pheasants are best in November / December. In cold weather, a phea-

sant should be hung for 10-14 days. In warm weather, 3-5 days. A pheasant will serve 3-4 depending on size.

Pigeon

Only wood-pigeons can be classified as game, although tame pigeons are also sold by some poulterers.

Like other young birds, young pigeons have downy feathers under the wings, soft, pliable legs and a supple breastbone. They may be bought ready prepared, but it is difficult to judge age unless you can feel the breastbone. Allow one bird per person. Pigeons should be hung for about two days.

Quail

Quail are the smallest of the British game birds. They are buff coloured with darker streaks. Quail are reared on game farms and are available all the year round. They are usually sold ready prepared. Because they are farm reared, you can be sure of getting a young quail. Quail are eaten undrawn. You will need one bird per person.

Guinea fowl

Guinea fowl are also farm reared and are available all the year round. The guinea fowl can be regarded as a sort of wild turkey as it tastes rather like turkey in flavour. Once again, it is safe to buy guinea fowl oven ready. One bird will serve 2-3 people.

Snipe, woodcock, plover

Snipe is a small, long-billed bird of the wader family. It does not appeal to most tastes because it is served whole, complete with head and bill. The flesh has quite a strong flavour. Woodcock and plover are similar. You are very unlikely to see these in poulterer's shops as conservationists are urging that these birds should not be shot. Because of the limited appeal, they are perhaps, best avoided.

PREPARING GAME BIRDS FOR ROASTING

If you buy your bird from a poulterer, he will hang, pluck and draw it for you (where appropriate). If you are given a bird, most poulterers will hang it for you and prepare it for roasting for a fee.

It is essential that game birds are hung, otherwise the true game flavour does not develop. The birds are hung from 2-10 days, depending on the weather. Hanging times are given in the section on individual birds so you can tell your butcher or poulterer how long you want your bird hung for.

More game birds, easily recognizable when feathered by their distinctive plumage. The birds shown are, from left to right: a wood-pigeon, a woodcock, a snipe (with its long pointed beak), a golden plover, a partridge and a guinea fowl (identified by its speckled grey plumage).

A rich, fruity stuffing goes particularly well with roasted game. This cranberry stuffing, although shown with grouse, can be used with many other birds as well.

STUFFING

Because game birds tend to be dry, a rich stuffing which will add moisture or, at the very least, some butter is always placed in the cavity. The amount of stuffing varies from bird to bird because they are all different sizes. It is best to check with individual recipes.

Like all other stuffings, those for game birds should not be prepared until just before required. They must be allowed to cool before being put in the bird. Nor should the bird be stuffed in advance.

To stuff the bird, first prepare your stuffing. Put the stuffing into the bird through the vent end, using a large spoon to fill the cavity in large birds and a smaller spoon to fill smaller birds. The bird should be loosely filled. When all the stuffing is in place, pull down the flap of skin above the vent and close the opening with small, thin poultry skewers. The opening at the neck end should be closed in the same way. This will trap the moisture inside the bird.

As well as the stuffings given here, you can try the stuffings given for duck and goose (pages 43 – 44) and turkey (pages 31 – 32).

An alternative to stuffing is to use flavoured butter. Lemon butter and orange butter, watercress butter and maître d'hotel butter are some of the best. You will need about 50 g [2 oz] butter for smaller birds, 75 g [3 oz] for larger.

●To make orange butter, first soften the butter until light and creamy. Blend in the grated zest and juice of an orange. Form into a ball and chill before putting inside the bird. Lemon butter is made in the same way.

●For watercress butter, soften the butter as for orange butter. Select about three good sprigs of watercress. Discard yellowing leaves and tough stalks. Chop the watercress finely and combine with the butter, adding a generous squeeze of lemon juice. Chill before use.

LIVER PATE STUFFING

 *The sherry added to this stuffing helps to bring out the flavour of the liver. This stuffing can also be used as a spread for toast. In the latter case, bake it in a buttered dish in a bain-marie in an oven set to 180°C [350°F] gas mark 4.*

FILLS ONE PHEASANT OR
TWO SMALL BIRDS
half an onion
50 g [2 oz] streaky bacon
15 g [½ oz] butter
150 g [5 oz] liver pâté
15 ml [1 tablespoon] sweet
   sherry or Madeira
salt
freshly ground black pepper
pinch of paprika

1 Skin the onion. Cut the rind off the bacon and mince or chop both finely.

2 Heat the butter in a small heavy-based pan. Fry the onion until soft and lightly coloured.

3 Add the bacon. Cook, stirring for a further 2 minutes. Drain off most of the fat.

4 In a bowl, cream the liver pâté with the sherry. Mix in the onion and bacon, plus the fat still remaining in the pan. Season to taste and stir in the paprika.

CREAM CHEESE STUFFING

This is a classic stuffing for pheasant. Always use full fat cream cheese to give a smooth, well-flavoured stuffing. If you do not have the bird's liver, a chicken liver may be used although the flavour will not be as good.

**FILLS ONE PHEASANT OR
TWO SMALLER BIRDS
half a small onion
1 pheasant or chicken liver
15 g [½ oz] butter
100 g [¼ lb] streaky bacon
15 ml [1 tablespoon] freshly
  chopped parsley
75 g [3 oz] full fat soft cheese
salt
freshly ground black pepper**

1 Skin and chop the onion. Wash the liver and discard any greenish parts. Chop finely or mince.

2 Heat the butter in a small heavy-based frying-pan. Fry onion and liver until the onion is soft but not coloured. Drain off the fat. Set aside.

3 Cut the rinds off the bacon. Cut the bacon into small pieces. Put in a bowl with the parsley. Stir in the onion and liver.

4 Add the cheese to the bowl. Mix all ingredients together well and season before use.

CRANBERRY STUFFING

Fruit is a traditional favourite with game and goes especially well with the strong, heather flavour of grouse. This stuffing may also be used with capercaillie, black game and partridge or guinea fowl.

**FILLS TWO GROUSE
175 g [6 oz] poached cranberries
25 g [1 oz] soft white
  breadcrumbs
15 g [½ oz] raisins
1.5 ml [¼ teaspoon] grated
  lemon zest
50 g [2 oz] butter
salt
freshly ground black pepper**

1 Drain the cranberries. Mix with breadcrumbs, raisins and zest.

2 Melt the butter. Stir into other ingredients. Season to taste.

BROWN RICE STUFFING

Although wild rice is traditional with game, it is now so expensive that very few cooks can afford to use it. Brown rice provides a pleasant alternative. This stuffing is excellent with pheasant and pigeon.

**FILLS TWO PHEASANTS OR
SIX PIGEONS
175 g [6 oz] cooked brown rice
30 ml [2 tablespoons] finely
  chopped onion
60 ml [4 tablespoons] chopped
  celery
15 ml [1 tablespoon] chopped
  green pepper
25 g [1 oz] chopped walnuts
25 g [1 oz] butter
livers of 2 pheasants or
  chickens
5 ml [1 teaspoon] freshly
  chopped parsley
pinch of dried marjoram
freshly ground black pepper**

1 Mix together the onion, celery, pepper and nuts.

2 Heat the butter in a heavy-based pan over low heat. Add the chopped vegetables and nuts and fry gently for 5 minutes.

3 Mix the contents of the pan into the rice. Chop the livers and add.

4 Stir in the parsley and marjoram. Add pepper to taste.

TRUSSING

After the bird has been stuffed, it must be trussed. Game birds may be trussed in the same way as described for chickens (see pages 16–17) with the exception of snipe and woodcock. These are skewered with their own long beaks through the back legs.

BARDING

Because game birds are naturally dry, extra fat must be added to prevent them drying out completely during roasting. The easiest way to do this is to wrap a sheet of pork fat or streaky bacon rashers, which you have stretched with the back of a knife, around the breast of the bird. Wrap the rashers around the bird, making sure they completely cover the breast and legs, then tie in place with string.

ROASTING

In order to prevent excessive drying out of the flesh, the barded game must be roasted at a high temperature. This means that cooking is fast.

Preparing the tin

To keep the bird moist and to help provide fat with which to baste during cooking, the tin in which the bird is roasted should be buttered generously. The tin should be quite a close fit round the bird—this will prevent the juices from spreading too thinly.

When the oven has reached the correct temperature (see chart), place the bird in the tin and position this in the centre of the oven. Cook for the time given on the chart, basting frequently with the pan juices or with extra melted butter if the pan juices are a bit sparse.

Frothing

About 5 minutes before the bird is ready, remove the bacon from the breast. Do not discard these crisp, pieces of bacon. They are useful for crumbling into soups or salads. Dredge the breast of the bird with flour. This will make the skin golden brown and crisp.

CARVING

Because game birds are small and often only serve one or two people, they are usually sold whole or halved. To halve a bird, simply cut down through the breastbone with a sharp

Step-by-step to roasting game birds

Bird	Temperature	Time per bird
Black grouse	220°C [425°F] gas mark 7	40 minutes
Capercaillie	as black grouse	40 minutes
Grouse	as black grouse	40 minutes
Guinea fowl	as black grouse	40 minutes
Partridge	as black grouse	25-30 minutes
Pigeon	230°C [450°F] gas mark 8	15 minutes
Plover	as black grouse	15-20 minutes
Pheasant	as black grouse	30 minutes
Ptarmigan	as black grouse	40 minutes
Quail	as black grouse	15 minutes
Snipe	as black grouse	15-20 minutes
Woodcock	as black grouse	15-20 minutes

1 Stuff the bird through the tail end with your chosen stuffing.

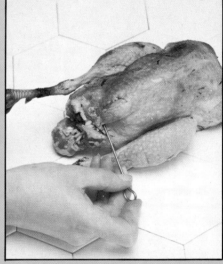

2 Secure the skin over the tail opening with a small poultry skewer.

5 Butter the roasting tin generously and place the bird in it.

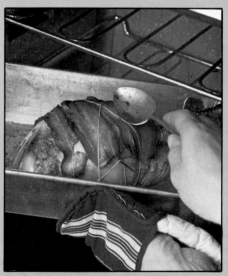

6 Cook the bird in the centre of the oven for the time given on the chart, basting often.

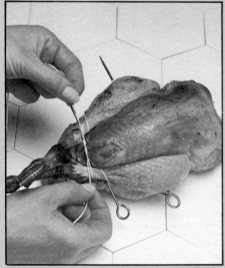

3 Truss the bird in the same way as you would truss a chicken, using small skewers.

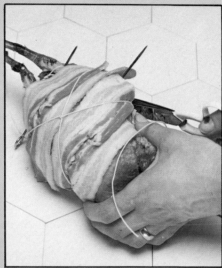

4 Tie thin sheets of pork fat or stretched streaky bacon rashers over the breast and legs.

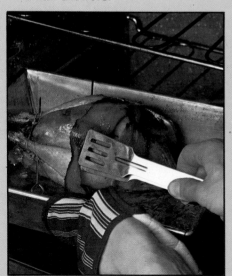

7 About 5 minutes before the bird is ready, remove the bacon from the breast.

8 Dredge the breast with plain flour. Return the bird to the oven and allow breast to brown.

knife and then chop through the backbone with a cleaver or cut with poultry shears.

ACCOMPANIMENTS FOR ROASTED GAME

Fruit sauces are a traditional and delicious accompaniment to game. Cranberry is perhaps the best known but apple, gooseberry and apricot are also good. Crab-apple jelly, if available, is excellent. Bread sauce (see page 22) may also be served.

Gravy for game is traditionally thin and has a base of giblet stock (see details on page 59). Two suitable suitable gravies given in the recipe section.

Bread in the form of croûte or fried crumbs is a well-known accompaniment for game. A croûte is usually served with small birds, while fried crumbs are served with larger birds such as pheasant or guinea fowl.

Making a croûte

A croûte is a slice of toasted or fried white bread about 2.5 cm [1"] thick. The bird is served on top of the croûte.

To make a croûte, remove the crusts from a thick slice of bread. Toast or fry in butter until pale golden. If you are serving a croûte with a bird, remove the tin from the oven about 10 minutes before the end of roasting. Lift the bird and slip it on to a roasting rack. The croûte then goes under the rack and juices from the bird drip down on to it. If wished, the liver of the bird may be minced and spread on the croûte before it is placed under the bird.

Fried crumbs

Fried crumbs are the other popular alternative to serve with roast game. They are usually served separately. To make fried crumbs, simply fry soft, fresh white breadcrumbs in butter until golden brown.

Other accompaniments.

The traditional vegetable accompaniment for game birds is game chips. Peel and cut potatoes into very thin rounds and deep-fry in hot oil. Drain and serve sprinkled with salt.

Roast potatoes are good with all game. Other suitable vegetables are Brussels sprouts, braised celery, turnips, swede, carrots or parsnips.

Watercress is frequently used to garnish a roast bird.

THIN GRAVY FOR GAME

This basic gravy makes good use of the tasty pan juices and of giblet stock. When you are making giblet stock, set the livers aside for use in making stuffings or for spreading on croûtes.

MAKES 575 ML [1 PT]
**giblets of 2 game birds or
   chickens
feet of 2 game birds or
   chickens (optional)
1 carrot
1 onion
bouquet garni
salt
freshly ground black pepper
2.5 ml [½ teaspoon] plain
   flour**

1   Wash the giblets. Scald the feet for 4 minutes in boiling water.

2   Put feet and giblets into a large saucepan. Scrub and slice the carrot. Skin and chop the onion and add both to the pan.

3   Just cover the ingredients with cold water and bring to the boil. Skim. Add bouquet garni and seasoning and simmer for 40 minutes.

4   Strain the stock. There should be about 700 ml [1¼ pt]. Remove the bird from the roasting tin and pour off the fat, leaving juices and sediment behind.

5   Sprinkle the flour into the tin. Stir into the sediment. Place over low heat and cook gently for 2–3 minutes, scraping the sediment from the bottom of the tin.

6   Remove from the heat and gradually stir in the giblet stock. Place over high heat and boil for 2–3 minutes. Season to taste if wished. Strain and serve.

RICH GRAVY FOR GAME

This very rich gravy makes game into a really special dish. It can very well be made in bulk and frozen if wished. It will keep for 3 months.

MAKES 275 ML [½ PT]
**450 g [1 lb] game or chicken
   giblets
225 g [½ lb] shin of beef
1 medium-sized onion**

**1 small carrot
15 g [½ oz] beef dripping
150 ml [¼ pt] beef stock
bouquet garni
salt
freshly ground black pepper**

1   Wash the giblets and set the livers aside for other use.

2   Blanch the giblets for 2 minutes in boiling water. Drain and rinse under cold water. Pat dry.

3   Cut the giblets and shin of beef into small pieces. Place in a heavy-based saucepan.

4   Skin and slice the onion. Scrub and chop the carrot. Add to pan.

5   Add the dripping to the pan. Melt slowly over low heat, turning the meat and vegetables so that they are coated in fat. Cook for about 5 minutes, until the onion is soft but not coloured.

6   Add the stock. Cook, stirring from time to time for about 15 minutes until the liquid has almost reduced to a glaze.

7   Pour in 700 ml [1¼ pt] cold water. Add the bouquet garni. Stir. Bring to the boil then reduce heat so that the liquid is just simmering. Half cover the pan.

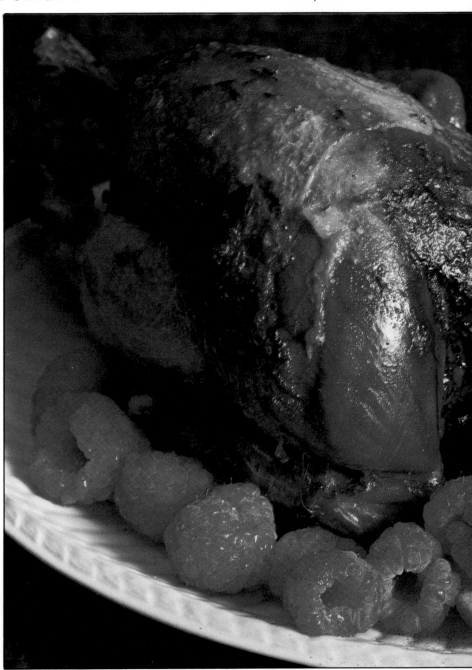

8 Simmer for 40 minutes until well reduced. Season to taste with salt and pepper.

9 Strain into a bowl and leave until cold. Lift off the fat. Heat before serving until throughly warmed through.

GROUSE WITH APPLE AND RASPBERRIES

The tart flavours of apples and raspberries provide an excellent contrast to the heathery tang of grouse. Frozen raspberries are fine for this dish but not canned ones as they are too sweet. Make lemon butter as shown on page 50.

SERVES 2
1 grouse weighing about 900 g [2 lb]
salt
freshly ground black pepper
25 g [1 oz] lemon butter
2 rashers streaky bacon
25 g [1 oz] butter
2 crisp dessert apples
100 g [¼ lb] frozen raspberries
15 ml [1 tablespoon] caster sugar
15 ml [1 tablespoon] melted butter
25 g [1 oz] plain flour
275 ml [½ pt] giblet stock

1 Wipe the grouse. Season inside and out. Place the lemon butter in the body cavity. Truss. Lay the bacon rashers over the breast.

2 Heat the oven to 220°C [425°F] gas mark 7. Butter a roasting tin.

3 Place the grouse in the tin. Cook in the centre of the oven for 40 minutes.

4 Peel and core the apples. Cut into thick slices. Toss raspberries in sugar and leave to thaw.

5 Place the apples in a baking tin. Pour the melted butter over them. About 20 minutes before the grouse will be ready, place the apples in the bottom of the oven.

6 Five minutes before the end of cooking, remove the bacon from the birds. Dredge with half of the flour and leave to brown.

7 Remove bird from the oven. Make gravy using pan juices, giblet stock and remaining flour.

8 Arrange the apple slices around the bird. Spoon on raspberries.

ROAST BRANDIED GUINEA FOWL

Guinea fowl is milder in flavour than other game birds because it is farm bred. The addition of brandy gives it the extra flavour needed. Serve it with buttered crumbs, watercress and apple sauce.

SERVES 4
2 guinea fowl weighing about 900 g [2 lb] each
salt and pepper
25 g [1 oz] chilled butter
2 streaky bacon rashers
25 g [1 oz] softened butter
275 ml [½ pt] giblet stock
30 ml [2 tablespoons] crushed juniper berries
30 ml [2 tablespoons] brandy
15 g [½ oz] plain flour

1 Wipe the birds. Season inside and out with salt and pepper. Put half the chilled butter inside each bird. Truss. Place bacon over the breasts.

2 Set the oven to 220°C [425°F] gas mark 7. Use the softened butter to grease the roasting tin.

55

3 Pour half the stock into the roasting tin. Place the birds in the tin. Roast for 10 minutes.

4 Add the crushed juniper berries, scattering them over the birds. Baste the birds with the stock.

5 Roast the birds for the time given in the roasting chart, basting frequently. Remove the bacon 5 minutes before the end of cooking.

6 When the birds are ready, warm the brandy. Pour over the birds and set alight.

7 When the flames have died down, remove the birds from the tin to a heated serving dish.

8 Make the gravy using the remaining stock, flour and pan juices as given in thin gravy for game birds (see page 54).

TRADITIONAL ROAST PHEASANT WITH GRAPES

It is traditional to garnish a pheasant with its own tail feathers just before bringing it to the table. Obviously if you do this, you cannot portion the bird in the kitchen. In this recipe, the breast of the bird is buttered to make it extra rich.

SERVES 2–3
pheasant weighing about 1.15 kg [2½ lb]
175 g [6 oz] white grapes
5 ml [1 teaspoon] grated lemon zest
salt
freshly ground black pepper
15 g [½ oz] softened butter
1 large rasher streaky bacon
425 ml [¾ pt] cold giblet stock
15 g [½ oz] plain flour

For the garnish:
fried breadcrumbs

1 Skin, halve and de-seed the grapes. Mix with the grated lemon zest. Set the oven to 220°C [425°F] gas mark 7.

2 Sprinkle the pheasant inside and out with salt and freshly ground black pepper.

3 Fill the pheasant with grapes, reserving any surplus for garnish.

4 Truss the pheasant as shown in step-by-step to roasting game birds. Cover the breast with butter. Tie the bacon rasher over the breast. Place in a roasting tin.

5 Pour all but 150 ml [¼ pt] of the cold stock over the pheasant.

6 Put the roasting tin in the centre of the oven. Roast for 30 minutes, basting frequently.

7 Five minutes before the end of cooking, remove the bacon and dredge the flour over the bird. Allow to brown.

8 Place the bird on a heated serving dish. Make the gravy as given for thin gravy, using the remaining stock and the sediment from the pan.

9 To garnish the bird, tie the quill ends of the feathers with fine thread. Insert a small poultry skewer into the bundle. Stick the skewer into the bird where the tail feathers should be so that they stick up.

ROAST PARTRIDGES WITH JUNIPER STUFFING

The delicate flesh of these small birds is delicious combined with juniper, which is the classic spice for game. If you select very small birds, you can serve one per person. This always looks more attractive than portions, however neatly carved.

Because there is stock in the pan there is no need to butter it to keep the birds moist.

SERVES 4
4 young partridges about 275 g [10 oz] each
4 streaky bacon rashers
50 g [2 oz] melted butter
350 ml [12 fl oz] giblet stock
25 g [1 oz] plain flour
salt
freshly ground black pepper

For the stuffing:
6 juniper berries
40 g [1½ oz] white bread
50 g [2 oz] cooked ham
1 medium-sized onion, skinned
5 ml [1 teaspoon] grated orange zest
pinch of marjoram

50 g [2 oz] melted butter
1 large egg
salt
freshly ground black pepper

For the croûtes:
4 slices white bread at least 2.5 cm [1"] thick
50 g [2 oz] butter
livers of the birds

1 Heat the oven to 220°C [425°F] gas mark 7.

2 Make the stuffing first. Crush the juniper berries. Mince together the bread, ham and onion.

3 Mix the minced ingredients with other stuffing ingredients, blending thoroughly.

4 Stuff and truss the birds. Lay the bacon rashers over the breasts.

5 Put the birds in a roasting tin. Trickle melted butter over them then pour over three-quarters of the stock.

6 Roast in the centre of the oven for 20 minutes, basting frequently with the stock.

7 When you have put the birds in the oven, start preparing the croûtes. Melt the butter in a heavy-based frying-pan. Cut the crusts off the bread and fry until golden.

8 Mince the livers and spread over the slices of fried bread.

9 Ten minutes before the end of roasting, raise the birds on to a roasting rack. Place the croûtes underneath.

10 Five minutes before the end of roasting, remove bacon and dredge the birds with some of the flour.

11 When the birds are cooked, place each on a croûte on a heated serving dish.

12 Use remaining giblet stock and flour to make thin gravy as given in thin gravy for game birds. Season to taste before serving.

A traditional roast pheasant and, in the background, a plate of stuffed partridges.

56

Flavour of the wild

Game was man's first meat and although we no longer depend on it for survival, it can make a delicious change to the farmed meat to which we have become accustomed. Cooks in castles and cottages have, throughout the ages, developed dishes of excellence which make good use of a source of meat still plentiful in season but often neglected.

Game is a meat that tends to be ignored, thanks to the swift transport and freezing that has made farmed meat so easy to obtain. Not only is this a waste of a natural source of food that has served man for many centuries, but the meat has a distinctive flavour which, with a little careful preparation, can be brought out to the full by roasting, braising, casseroling or stewing. Any leftovers can be used to make pies and pâtés and the bonier parts used for soups and stock.

Explained here are techniques of roasting game. The stages of preparation which can be easily carried out at home are the marinating, stuffing, trussing and barding. The preliminary stages of preparation, that is hanging, paunching and skinning may be done at home, but will also be done by a kindly butcher, on request, if you buy a whole, unprepared animal. Many are available which have been completely prepared before sale.

TYPES OF GAME ANIMAL

The types of game animal most commonly found and cooked are rabbit, hare and venison. Several other animals such as hedgehog, squirrel and boar, are eaten as game meat on the European continent and in other parts of the world, and bear and beaver are eaten in the colder parts of North America and in Canada.

Rabbit

There are two types of rabbit, wild and tame (farmed), both available from suppliers of game. The meat of each is quite different.

Wild rabbit has been popular with cooks throughout history, proof that the meat makes better eating than it is now given credit for. The flesh is dark with a noticeable game flavour, which is affected by its diet. A rabbit that has fed in a cornfield will be particularly plump and well flavoured.

Tame rabbits (so-called) are now farmed in quantity, both for their pelts and their meat. They have white flesh, are a good deal larger than wild rabbits and are more expensive.

Hare

Hare is found all over the world and has been associated with folk tales since ancient times. The Romans maintained that eating hare made one beautiful! In most parts of Europe and the Far East, hare is valued as a luxury meat. The British are almost alone in treating it as fit only for everyday eating. It is in season from the beginning of August to the end of February in the northern hemisphere.

There are two types of hare. The larger, and the tastier, is the lowland brown hare of central and southern Europe, introduced into Australasia. The second type is the Scottish blue hare, which may be the same creature as the Arctic hare found in North America. Other types of American hare are known as snow-shoe and jack rabbits.

The flesh of hare becomes darker the older the animal is. A young hare, with lighter coloured and less game flavoured flesh, is called a leveret.

Venison

In days gone by, any wild animal used for food was called venison; in English-speaking countries the term is now only used for the flesh of deer and similar animals, such as the reindeer, moose, elk, buck and caribou.

Three types of deer are commonly found in Great Britain: red deer, roe deer and fallow deer. The three varieties are treated for cooking in the same way.

The red deer is the most noble British game animal but the meat of fallow deer is held by gourmets to have the finest flavour. Roe deer meat is whiter in colour and less game flavoured. Buck meat is considered to be better than that of the doe (the female). As with game birds, venison has a close season, when the animals may not be shot. Fresh venison is available in the northern hemisphere from June–September (bucks) and October–December (does). The animals are at their best for eating between 18 months and 3 years old.

CHOOSING AND BUYING GAME ANIMALS

Although deer, rabbits and hares are shot in the wild, most people have to buy their game meat. If you buy a joint, the animal will have already been paunched (that is, the innards removed) and skinned and the meat hung. A whole rabbit will have been paunched and hung but may still be in its skin. A hare will have been hung but will not necessarily have been skinned and paunched. Although

these tasks are not difficult, they are not appealing to everyone, are time consuming and take some care and attention. The butcher from whom you purchase the game will skin and paunch the animal for you.

It is most important though to be able to assess what you are buying, at whatever stage of preparation it has reached. You also need to know the further treatment which may be necessary before cooking, which differs with the age of the animal and its condition.

Rabbits, wild and farmed

Rabbits can be bought whole or jointed. If you are roasting, which is the subject of this course, you will need to buy a whole animal. Wild and farmed rabbits can be bought already prepared, that is paunched, hung and skinned, or simply paunched and hung, but not skinned.

If you buy the wholly prepared rabbit, the hints as to age and condition, which are obvious in an animal still in its skin, will not be there. Look for plump flesh, plenty of fat around the kidneys and a bright red liver. These giblets will be left in the carcass with the heart, as with a chicken.

Wild rabbits, still in their skins and hanging by their hind legs, are a common sight in the window of a game butcher. If you buy one of these animals you will be better able to judge its age and condition. Look for a pliable lower jaw, small, even white teeth, a narrow lip cleft and thin soft ears which would tear easily. The feet should be flexible with smooth, sharp claws and the pads underneath well developed. All these are signs of a young rabbit. A rabbit with thick haunches, rough blunt claws and dry ears is probably too old for anything but stew or stock.

A wild rabbit is a fairly small animal, the average weight after preparation for cooking being 1 kg [2¼ lb] which will serve 4–5 people. Its handling and cooking is like that of a young hare. The average weight of a farmed rabbit after preparation is about 1.4 kg [3 lb] serving 4–6 people and the big Ostend type is even larger and may weigh up to 2.9 kg [6½ lb]. Farmed rabbits, although their meat is less delicate than that of chicken, are handled and can be cooked in most of the ways suitable for chicken.

Joints of both wild and farmed rabbits are sold fresh and frozen. Fresh saddle and hindquarter joints, with their fleshier meat, may be more expensive than . the bonier forequarter joints. You can buy a joint for each member of the family, as you would chicken joints.

Frozen rabbit is quite widely available; most of it is imported, farmed rabbit, pale pink in colour. You can buy frozen rabbit not only as joints, but also in blocks of boneless rabbit meat. This frozen boneless meat seems solid when you buy it still frozen, but do not expect to be able to cook it 'in the piece' like a frozen fish steak. It breaks up into small pieces when thawed.

Frozen rabbit needs some care in preparation and cooking; otherwise it can be tasteless and tough. The boneless meat in particular is better used for making stews and casseroles.

Hares
Like all game, hares make better eating when young. A hare is at its best for the table between 3–6 months old, although a female (doe) may still be tender at 18 months.

Hares are sold like rabbits, whole and unprepared, whole and completely prepared or in joints. A hare is

hung to tenderize it before its head, feet and fur are removed and before it is paunched. Many game butchers then sell the animals as they are, and will prepare the animal as requested. This is the best buy as you can really see what you are getting. The following signs will help you to choose well, if you are buying a whole, unprepared hare.

A young hare can be identified by its short stumpy neck, long slender joints, smooth sharp claws hidden by fur and its small white teeth; its coat is smooth, its ears soft and its lip cleft narrow. As the animal ages, its claws project and become rounded and rough, the lip cleft widens, its teeth become long, irregular and yellow and its coat coarsens. Grey flecks appear in the coat, white hairs appear around the animal's muzzle and its ears become dry and tough.

Hares that are sold unskinned are generally sold at a fixed price, regardless of weight. The animal will lose up to 40 per cent of its weight by the time it is ready for cooking. The lowland brown hare will weigh about 2.2–4 kg [5–9 lb] when prepared and the smaller Scottish blue, 1.4–2.7 kg [3–6 lb]. A whole brown hare, stuffed will serve 8–10 people and a Scottish blue or a leveret, 5–6 people.

If you buy a hare already skinned it may be whole or in joints. A good reason for buying the whole animal is that the liver, heart and kidneys are left in place when the animal is paunched. These are valuable for making rich stock, or can be used in a grilled supper dish. Another very good reason for buying the whole animal is the blood. The blood collects in a membrane under the ribs while the animal is hanging and makes a rich thickening for the gravy, or a sauce. You can ask the butcher to partially joint the animal for you at purchase. As well as asking for the blood (which will come sealed in a separate bag and will not be poured in on top of the joints) also ask for the head and trimmings. You will have paid for these and be entitled to them. You can then use the body, in a piece, for roasting and use the other joints in a stew.

If you buy joints of hare you are obviously not entitled to the trimmings and the blood. The saddle and the hindquarters (the rabble) are the best parts of the animal for roasting and are roasted in the piece. The forelegs, or wings as they are called,

are best made into a civet (hare stew), although in a young leveret may be tender enough to be roasted. The flesh of the animal gets darker with age and in an old animal may be almost purple.

Venison
Venison is sold already hung, skinned and jointed. It is very important, for tenderness and flavour, that venison is properly hung and then marinated before cooking, or it will be flavourless, dry and tough. If you buy from a game butcher who buys his meat privately, he will willingly tell you how long it has been hung and its probable degree of game flavour. He will tell you how long you should marinate it before cooking to complete the tenderizing and flavouring process. The meat of a fawn, up to about 18 months old, is more tender but the game flavour is virtually undetectable. However, if you buy from a large store you will have to choose the meat just by its appearance. Stewing meat is usually sold chopped into small pieces and can also be bought frozen. Take no chances when buying a roasting joint. Even if it is sold as ready for roasting, it is always wise to marinate it, as shown here, before cooking it.

The flesh of venison should be dark, fine-grained, with thick, firm, clear white fat. The best joints are, in order, the haunch, the saddle, the loin and the shoulder. The remaining joints should not be roasted but used for stewing. If possible, choose a joint not damaged by shot, because torn or ragged meat deteriorates quickly.

A haunch is the classic roasting joint but will probably be too large for the average family. Part of the loin is a good buy; have some of it cut into chops. When buying, calculate the weight required by allowing 175–200 g [7–8 oz] per serving.

STORAGE
Do not try to store newly-killed game or fresh game bought from a shop. The only game that can be stored successfully is the rabbit and venison bought frozen. The meat can be stored for up to 6 months.

Fresh game from a game butcher, market or shop which has been bought already hung, paunched and skinned, should be put into a marinade immediately. The outer flesh on

all the animals will harden otherwise and will dry out. Hare, with its valuable blood can be particularly messy and must be dealt with immediately.

Frozen rabbit or venison should be thawed slowly in the refrigerator taking between 12–24 hours. Once defrosted, venison should be put into a marinade straight away; rabbit should be soaked and then marinated.

Cooked game, although it can be used in other dishes, is not worth storing. The meat does not keep well and becomes dry and stringy. The best use for leftovers is to make them, fairly promptly, into one of the excellent traditional pâtés to which game lends its flavour so well.

PREPARING GAME ANIMALS FOR ROASTING

The meat of game animals, particularly venison, tends to be dry and for this reason is greatly improved by being marinated before being cooked. This is not necessary for farmed rabbit but is very important if venison or wild rabbit is to be roasted. The meat must be protected from the dry heat of the oven and the marinating,

barding and frequent basting all help to do this.

In addition to marinating, rabbits, both wild and farmed, must be rinsed and soaked as soon as possible after skinning. This neutralizes any very strong flavour and lightens the colour of the flesh.

The first thing to do with a hare is to carefully transfer the blood into a bowl. The blood will most likely have been sealed in a plastic bag by the butcher. If not, and it is still inside the animal, puncture the membrane under the ribs which encloses the blood and drain it into a bowl.

Once the game has been marinated, rabbits and hares can be stuffed and trussed ready for cooking. Venison is not stuffed but must be trimmed of fat and all the joints must be well barded.

Soaking a rabbit

As soon as you get the skinned rabbit home, remove the giblets and rinse the animal several times in lightly salted water. Then fill a bowl with clean salted water and leave the rabbit to soak, completely immersed, for at least 30 minutes. Pat the rabbit dry after removing it from the water and then marinate it.

Rabble of hare—a succulent dish of roasted meat served with a creamy sauce.

Marinating game animals

All game meat is improved by a period of marinating before cooking as this continues the tenderizing process which has been started by the hanging, and adds moisture to the meat. For venison, marinating is an essential part of the preparation for roasting.

The most usual marinade used is one made with red wine, which has been cooked. Basic marinade including wine and vinegar is adapted by replacing the vinegar with extra wine and it can be made with red or white wine. The marinade must be cooked before use if it is to be used for longer than 24 hours. The marinade should include 15–30 ml [1–2 tablespoons] wine vinegar, the only concession to a great size being an increase in the quantity of vinegar used. Use a non-corrosive vessel and one that is large enough to allow the meat to be turned in the marinade, from time to time.

Wild rabbit: if it is young and has been soaked properly it may not necessarily need marinating. However, as marinating can only

61

improve the meat, it is worth the very small amount of work. Put a young animal to soak in red wine to which you have added 15 ml [1 tablespoon] vinegar, or in white wine with 15 ml [1 tablespoon] lemon juice, according to your recipe. For example, do not soak the animal in red wine if white wine is used during cooking, and vice versa.

An older, probably more tough, animal and frozen rabbit meat which can be rather flavourless can be marinated with a marinade made up of wine as suggested above and made with white wine and used uncooked. Marinate the animal for 2 hours and this will greatly improve the flavour of a frozen rabbit and the quality of a tougher animal.

Hare: a hare should, like venison, always be marinated before cooking to ensure tenderness and flavour. Use a recipe, suitably adapted making it with red wine. Cook the marinade before soaking the animal and use 20 ml [4 teaspoons] vinegar Leave the animal to marinate for 12 hours, or longer if the hare is rather old and stringy.

A young hare (leveret) does not need to be soaked in a liquid marinade. Sprinkle the animal with dried herbs, selecting them to complement those used in the recipe for cooking. Then sprinkle the animal with 75 ml [3 fl oz] oil and equal quantities (30 ml [2 tablespoons]) water with either vinegar, red wine, white wine or brandy. Leave the leveret to absorb the flavours for 3–4 hours.

Venison: even the better joints of venison which are used for roasting must always be marinated before cooking. Correct hanging is also essential for tenderness and flavour and although your meat will already have been hung by your supplier, this may not have been sufficient for your liking. Marinating is a continuation of the hanging process and the longer the meat is marinated the stronger the game flavour and the more tender the meat. A marinade also prevents the meat from deteriorating.

Cover the venison with a cooked, red wine marinade following a suitable recipe which is adapted, using 30 ml [2 tablespoons] vinegar. Leave the joint to soak for 24–48 hours, turning from time to time. After 24 hours the meat will be tender and the longer that it is left after this, the greater the game flavour will be. It is perfectly

safe to leave the meat for a further 24 hours (72 hours in total) if you wish a really distinctive game flavour.

Stuffing
Hare and rabbit can be roasted with or without stuffing. If not stuffed, the stuffing mixture can be shaped into balls and served as an accompaniment. Several stuffings are used with hare and rabbit: those used with chicken (see page 16) and for game birds (see page 50). The stuffings often contain fat meat or fruit to enrich and flavour the rather dry meat.

The animals are stuffed in the body cavity created by paunching. Spoon the stuffing into the cavity until it is full but not packed too tightly. Then draw the edges of the cavity together and sew up with strong thread (not nylon or plastic coated). Leave a long end to the thread so that it can be pulled out after cooking, without touching the hot meat.

You will need about 175 g [6 oz] stuffing for a rabbit to serve four people. A hare, which will serve six, will take about 350 g [¾ lb] stuffing.

Venison is not stuffed. The joints are large and the meat solid so extra bulk is unnecessary. Nor does the savoury flesh require the extra flavour that stuffing provides.

Trussing and barding
Game animals can be roasted in joints or whole. When roasted whole, stuffed or unstuffed, they need to be trussed in order to hold their shape.
Rabbit and hare: a whole rabbit or a hare is trussed in the same way, except for the head, and the process is very straightforward.

In both animals, the forelegs are pulled backwards along the side of the body. The hind legs are then pulled forward which necessitates cutting through the sinew in the thigh. The legs should overlap slightly and can be held in place by a poultry skewer. This is all that is necessary with an animal that is served without its head.

If you are trussing an animal with the head in place, there are two methods of securing it. One is to turn the head sideways and twist it so that it can be skewered to the breast or shoulder. Alternatively, with a young hare that is being trussed in the traditional style, the head is held

upright. Push a poultry skewer down through the lower jaw and into the front of the neck. Then tie a string to the leg skewer on one side of the animal, pass it through the skewer in the jaw and tie off at the leg skewer on the other side. This will hold the head securely in place.

A hare can also be roasted with the forequarters removed. This makes a good-sized roast for six people and the rest of the hare is used for another dish. The forequarters are cut off just behind the shoulder and the saddle, haunches and hind legs are roasted in a piece.

The backbone of a hare is very tough and if you are removing the forequarters you will need a very sharp heavy knife or a pair of poultry shears in order to cut through the backbone. The forequarters can be kept and used for a stew or stock. The hind legs are trussed in the same way as with a whole animal and are secured to the side of the animal with poultry skewers.

Rabbits and hares need to be well barded before being put in the oven. Use plenty of fat bacon and lay the rashers over the animal to cover the body. If the head is still in place, cover this with several layers of greased foil and do the same with the legs if the bacon does not cover them completely.

Venison: joints of venison should be trimmed, and then barded or covered with foil before being roasted. Trim any ragged ends from the meat and all fibres and fat. The taste of deer fat is unpleasant and affects the flavour of the meat. The meat is, however, dry so the lack of fat must be compensated for by generous barding. Use plenty of fat bacon laid across the whole joint or cover the surface of the joint with softened fat and lay a double thickness of foil over the top. If a haunch joint still has the hind leg attached, wrap the latter in several layers of greased foil.

This generous barding or the fat and foil covering, combined with frequent basting will keep the joint moist during cooking.

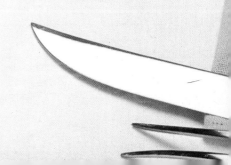

ROASTING GAME ANIMALS

The most important point to remember when roasting rabbit, hare and venison is that the meat must be kept moist throughout cooking. The meat must be well barded or protected with foil before being put in the oven.

Roasting rabbit and hare

Wild rabbit and hare are roasted in exactly the same way, for the same length of time, despite their difference in size. A farmed rabbit should be trussed and barded like a wild rabbit and then roasted in the same way as a chicken (see pages 18 – 19).

Sit the prepared hare or rabbit on a roasting rack. Place it in a roasting tin with any fat or liquid that your recipe includes. Roast the animal at 220°C [425°F] gas mark 7 for 10–15 minutes. Reduce the oven temperature to 180°C [350°F] gas mark 4 and continue roasting the animal for a further 35–40 minutes. Baste the meat frequently and generously and after 30 minutes total cooking, remove the barding bacon or foil to allow the meat to brown. Continue basting the meat frequently. Test the meat to see if it is cooked after 40 minutes. Push a thin skewer into the thickest part of the haunch above the thigh, and if it comes out clean and no blood seeps from the flesh, the meat is cooked.

If you are roasting only the saddle and haunches of a hare, it will still take the same time to cook as a whole animal. Roast it at the same temperature, basting frequently and test for readiness after 40 minutes.

Roasting venison

Venison is the driest of all game animals and must be very thoroughly barded and protected from the dry heat of the oven. Venison can be fast or slow roasted but the fast roasting method can only be recommended for properly hung, tender animals, when the results will be excellent. If you do not know for certain for how long the animal was hung or have any doubts about its quality, it is better to slow roast the meat.

If you are fast roasting, set the oven to 220°C [425°F] gas mark 7 and roast your joint for 12–15 minutes per 450 g [1 lb]. Roast it on a rack in a roasting tin and baste generously throughout cooking. Remove the barding or foil 15 minutes from the end of cooking and allow the surface to brown. Continue basting while browning.

The slow roasting method is obviously a rather lengthy process but it will ensure that the meat is tender and juicy when cooked. Roast the meat for 40 minutes per 450 g [1 lb] at 160°C [325°F] gas mark 3. Baste the meat frequently and remove the barding or foil about 20 minutes before the end of the calculated cooking time to allow the surface to brown. This final browning can be increased by dredging the joint with plain flour before returning it to the oven. The flour will 'froth' and brown.

CARVING GAME ANIMALS

Game meat cools quickly, particularly venison, and the flavour of the meat is affected. The joint, or animal should not, therefore, be rested in the normal way but served immediately.

Venison can be carved in exactly the same way as a similar type of joint of lamb or mutton. Venison meat is close knit and will carve thinly even without the 'resting' period.

Both hare and rabbit are awkward to carve and jointing is the most efficient and satisfactory way of portioning the meat. This can be done in the kitchen or at table, although if done behind the scenes it allows you to keep the portioned meat hot while dealing with the rest. If dealing with a hare, have a pair of poultry shears handy to deal with the very tough backbone. If the animal was roasted with a stuffing, remove this by pulling out the thread by the long end and spooning out the stuffing. Serve it on a separate dish if serving from the kitchen, or in spoonfuls with each portion of meat at table.

First, cut the forequarters, with the legs attached, from the rest of the animal cutting through just behind the shoulders. With a rabbit, simply divide in half, but with a hare, cut the

legs from the forequarters, cutting round the shoulder joint and taking some of the flesh with the leg. This gives you two leg portions and a forequarter portion.

You are now left with the saddle and the haunches with the hind legs attached. In a rabbit, this is three or four portions. Cut the saddle from the haunches and cut the haunches in two, down the middle. For four portions, cut the saddle in half. A hare, being larger, is divided into six portions. The saddle is divided in half to make two, then the hind legs are detached from the haunches, at the joint (two portions), and the haunches are cut in half with poultry shears (two portions).

TRADITIONAL ACCOMPANIMENTS

Prepare your accompaniments for roasted game either before cooking or while the meat is roasting. It is important to serve the meat, especially venison, while still really hot and juicy.

Roasted meat is always served with gravy or some variety of moistening sauce. Both rabbit and venison are served with an unthickened gravy in the same way as a traditional turkey (see page 34), but not so hare. Hare is traditionally served with a thick gravy which is made by adding the blood of the hare. This is why it is important to ask the butcher for the blood when buying the animal.

Thick or thin gravy is, however, a matter of personal taste and gravy can always be thickened, as when you serve a gravy with lamb. If you wish to serve something rather more adventurous than gravy with your meat, try a fruit sauce. Oranges and redcurrants in particular, go well with game, but any sweet-sour or tart fruit can be used for a sauce.

If you serve gravy with the meat, provide a bowl of redcurrant or any other sharp fruit-flavoured jelly as well.

If hare or rabbit is roasted without stuffing, the stuffing mixture can be shaped into balls, fried briefly and then cooked with the meat for the last 30 minutes of roasting.

Bacon rolls can be served with hare and rabbit. Also delicious are onions roasted with hare during cooking. Roast potatoes are a traditional accompaniment to all roast meat as are green vegetables or a salad.

FORCEMEAT STUFFING

Old in history, but reliable and tasty, this recipe comes from a cookery book of 1860. Use it either to stuff your hare, or to make into forcemeat balls. Fry the balls in lard until lightly browned on all sides or put in the roasting tin with the animal for the last 30 minutes of cooking. Baste well.

FOR A MEDIUM-SIZED HARE OR TWO RABBITS
50 g [2 oz] lean rindless bacon or cooked ham
100 g [$\frac{1}{4}$ lb] shredded suet
grated rind of half a lemon
5 ml [1 teaspoon] freshly chopped parsley
5 ml [1 teaspoon] freshly chopped mixed herbs or 2.5 ml [$\frac{1}{2}$ teaspoon] dried mixed herbs
salt
small pinch of cayenne pepper
pinch of ground mace
175 g [6 oz] soft white breadcrumbs
3 medium-sized eggs

1 Cut the bacon or ham into small pieces and shred or mince.

2 Put the bacon or ham, suet, grated lemon rind, parsley, herbs, salt, pepper and mace in a bowl.

3 Mix thoroughly with a fork, breaking up any lumps of suet.

4 Stir in the breadcrumbs. Make sure all the ingredients are evenly mixed.

5 Beat the eggs lightly in a small bowl. Mix them into the dry forcemeat gradually. Use enough egg to make a light firm mixture which you can roll into balls. It should not be sloppy.

THICKENED GRAVY FOR HARE

The gravy that is traditionally served with hare is thickened with beurre manié, the hare's liver and the blood. Use the other innards to make a stock (see page 18) and this will form the basis of your gravy. Use as much or as little of the hare's blood as you wish, but do not use more blood than stock. If you use less blood or find the resulting flavour, having used 425 ml [$\frac{3}{4}$ pt], too strong, add some extra stock.

SERVES 8–10
425 ml [$\frac{3}{4}$ pt] giblet stock
50 g [2 oz] butter
1 hare's liver
40 g [1$\frac{1}{2}$ oz] plain flour
425 ml [$\frac{3}{4}$ pt] hare's blood

1 Skim any fat from the surface of the cold strained stock. Put it to heat while the meat is still cooking.

2 When the meat is cooked, remove it and the rack from the roasting tin and keep hot. Pour the fat from the tin and put over a low heat.

3 Pour the hot stock into the tin, stirring and scraping any sediment from the bottom of the tin. Set aside.

4 Melt 15 g [$\frac{1}{2}$ oz] butter in a small frying-pan. Fry the liver gently over low heat, turning once, for a few minutes. It should be brown outside but still pink in the middle.

5 Tip the contents of the frying-pan into a bowl and mash the liver. Then pound it until smooth.

6 Bring the giblet stock in the roasting tin to the boil. While doing this use the remaining butter and the flour to make a beurre manié. Add this, in small pieces and over low heat, to the boiling stock. Stir to thicken and remove from the heat.

7 Stir in the pounded liver and as much blood as you wish. Heat gently without boiling and serve in a heated sauce-boat.

ROAST VENISON WITH APPLES

Young venison is so good for its price that it is well worth the treat of a roasted joint. The venison must be from either the saddle or the haunch and should be marinated before cooking. If you have no port, use the end of a bottle of medium-sweet red wine to make the gravy. Make the stock from a cube. Garnish with watercress.

SERVES 4

1 kg [2¼ lb] venison
45 ml [3 tablespoons] soft beef
   dripping
4 small cooking apples or
   Cox's orange pippins
juice of a lemon
15 g [½ oz] butter
45 ml [3 tablespoons]
   redcurrant jelly
10 ml [2 teaspoons] caster
   sugar
1 clove
175 ml [6 fl oz] beef stock
5 ml [1 teaspoon] salt

2.5 ml [½ teaspoon] freshly
   ground black pepper
2.5 ml [½ teaspoon] ground
   cinnamon
10 ml [2 teaspoons] cornflour
75 ml [3 fl oz] port

1 Heat the oven to 170°C [325°F] gas mark 3. Trim any ragged ends of the meat. Brush the meat all over with soft dripping and cover with a double thickness of foil.

2 Place the meat on a rack in a roasting tin and put in the oven. Baste about every 10 minutes while roasting, replacing the foil each time.

3 Prepare the apples. Peel and core them but keep them whole. Mix the lemon juice with 175 ml [6 fl oz] water and bring it to simmering point in a saucepan.

4 Put in the apples, and simmer very gently for 5 minutes. They should be tender outside but not broken. Drain and cool them.

5 Work the butter until soft with the back of a spoon. Work in 15 ml [1 tablespoon] jelly. Fill the mixture into the core holes in the apples. Top them with the sugar.

6 When the meat has been cooking for about 55 minutes, arrange the apples on the roasting rack beside the meat. Return to the oven and continue cooking.

7 For the final 20 minutes of cooking, remove the foil to allow the meat to brown. Baste well.

8 Crush the clove. Put the stock into a small saucepan. Scatter in the crushed clove. Add the remaining 30 ml [2 tablespoons] jelly, and the salt, pepper and cinnamon.

9 Bring the mixture slowly to the boil and stir until the jelly dissolves. Stir the cornflour into 15 ml [1 tablespoon] water, add a little hot stock and add to the pan. Simmer for 1 minute, stirring all the time. Put aside to keep warm.

10 When the meat is cooked, transfer it to a heated serving dish. Arrange the apples around it. Keep it hot while you finish the sauce.

11 Tilt the roasting tin. Skim off excess fat. Stir in the thickened stock. Mix well, scraping up and stirring in any sediment from the bottom of the tin.

12 Heat the sauce gently over low heat on top of the stove until very hot but not boiling. Stir in the port and serve in a heated sauce-boat.

ROAST STUFFED RABBIT

☒☒*The lightly flavoured flesh of a farmed rabbit does not need a strong stuffing. The lemony flavour of the forcemeat in this course suits it well, if you use freshly ground black pepper instead of cayenne—use half the quantity in the recipe. The chicken stock can, if wished, be made simply with a cube.*

SERVES 4–6
1.4 kg [3 lb] farmed rabbit, approximate weight when skinned and paunched
salt
20 ml [4 teaspoons] lemon juice
90 g [3½ oz] forcemeat stuffing
30 ml [2 tablespoons] French mustard
freshly ground black pepper
15 ml [1 tablespoon] cooking oil
4 rashers fat bacon
150 ml [¼ pt] chicken stock
freshly chopped parsley

1 Cut off the rabbit's head if still in place and take out the giblets.

2 Rinse the rabbit two or three times in lightly salted water. Then leave to soak, immersed in salted water with 5 ml [1 teaspoon] lemon juice added, for 30 minutes.

3 Wipe the rabbit and pat it dry. Stuff it with the forcemeat as described in this course.

4 Heat the oven to 190°C [375°F] gas mark 5.

5 Truss the rabbit with skewers, pulling the fore legs back and the hind legs forward.

6 Spread the mustard all over the rabbit. Sprinkle it with salt and pepper.

7 Place the rabbit on a rack in a roasting tin. Sprinkle it with the oil and the remaining lemon juice.

8 Cover the rabbit with the bacon. Trickle the stock over it.

9 Put the rabbit in the oven. Roast it for 40 minutes. Baste it frequently with the stock in the tin.

10 After 40 minutes, take bacon barding off the rabbit. Baste it with stock. Return it to the oven for 10–15 minutes or until lightly browned.

11 Place the rabbit on a heated serving dish. Pull or snip out the sewing thread. Keep the rabbit hot under buttered paper.

12 Tilt the roasting tin so that the juices run to one end. Skim off as much fat as you can. Scrape up and stir in any sediment from the bottom of the tin.

13 Put the tin over moderate heat, on top of the stove. Bring to the boil. Boil for 2 minutes. Check the flavour and seasoning.

14 Strain the gravy into a heated sauce-boat. Sprinkle the rabbit with chopped parsley. Serve at once.

GERMAN ROAST SADDLE AND RABBLE OF HARE

☒☒*You get the best of all worlds when using this recipe. Marinating and roasting with wine in the pan will give you tender meat, even from an old hare. Yet the cooking method is as simple as plain roasting. You have the pleasure of a roast joint and, as a luxurious bonus, the richness of a cream-finished sauce and mushrooms to go with it. Prepare the meat by removing the head and forequarters, taking out innards and marinating.*

SERVES 6
1 hare, weighing 2–2.25 kg [4½-5 lb] when skinned and paunched, marinated
6 rashers rindless streaky bacon
75 g [3 oz] dripping
275 ml [½ pt] red wine
225 g [½ lb] flat mushrooms
150 ml [¼ pt] soured cream
15 ml [1 tablespoon] cornflour
salt and pepper

1 Heat the oven to 220°C [425°F] gas mark 7.

2 Take the joint of hare from the marinade and pat dry carefully with kitchen paper. Truss the hind legs by pulling them forward and securing with skewers.

3 Place it on a rack in a roasting tin. Cover its back with the bacon rashers and the hind legs with some greased foil if the bacon does not cover them.

4 Heat the dripping gently until melted. Pour it over the hare.

5 Roast the hare for 15 minutes. Reduce the oven heat to 180°C [350°F] gas mark 4. Pour the wine into the roasting tin.

6 Continue roasting for another 40 minutes. Baste the joint with wine several times.

7 Add the mushrooms to the roasting rack, around the meat. Baste them well, remove the barding bacon and reserve. Roast the meat for another 10 minutes or until the hare is tender.

8 Put the joint, mushrooms and bacon on a heated serving dish. Keep hot. Blend cornflour with 30 ml [2 tablespoons] water.

9 Tilt the roasting tin, and skim off as much fat as you can from the sauce. Scrape up the sediment from the bottom of the tin. Stir in the soured cream.

10 Heat the sauce in the tin over low heat. Bring it to boiling point and add a little to the blended cornflour. Stir this mixture into the tin and boil for 1 minute. Season.

11 Portion the hare, making 2 portions from the saddle, 2 from the haunch and 1 each from the hind legs. Pour a little of the sauce over. Cut up the bacon and arrange this and the mushrooms on the serving dish. Serve the remaining sauce separately.

New rules for old game

As game gets older, it gets tougher, making the flesh totally unsuitable for roasting. This however, is not the end of the story. Using the tender techniques of casseroling and braising, you can turn even the toughest old bird or beast into a delicious meal.

Game, like other things (including people), gets tougher as it gets older. As every good cook knows, meat which is past the first tender flush of youth needs slow, persuasive cooking to make it tasty and succulent. Gentle casseroling and braising are ideal methods for this purpose and are excellent ways to cook end of season game birds, hare, rabbit and the tougher cuts of venison.

Long slow cooking will give these tougher beasts a new succulence. Casseroles provide more liquid whereas braises include more vegetables and less liquid.

Generally speaking, game is best when cooked with alcohol of some kind. Replace up to half the liquid with wine, cider or beer. The alcohol will evaporate during cooking leaving behind a subtle flavour. Wine and cider will reduce during cooking whereas beer will not, so casseroles made with beer are thickened at the end of cooking time.

GAME TO USE
All game can be braised or casseroled but this method is only worthwhile for older birds, hare, rabbit and the stewing cuts of venison.

Birds
With birds, it is fairly easy to detect age if they are sold feathered. The feathers under the wings will be fully formed rather than downy, cock pheasants will have pronounced spurs and the scales on the legs and feet of all birds will be larger and coarser than those of young specimens. The feet, beak and breastbone of old birds are rigid rather than pliable and in old partridges, the legs are red rather than yellow. If the birds are sold ready dressed, you can only take the butcher's word for their age but it is worth betting that any birds sold towards the end of the game season (see details on page 48) for

game seasons in the UK) will be beyond the age when they can be roasted successfully. With pigeons, it is hard to judge age anyway and they are almost always better casseroled or braised than roasted.

Rabbit and hare
It is difficult to judge the age of rabbit and hare. The only guideline that can be relied on is the ears. If the ears are soft and will tear easily, the animal is young. If they are tough, the animal is old. With cut rabbit it is impossible to judge age so here it is best to play safe and casserole or braise rather than roast.

Venison
Venison is sold ready-cut and is usually clearly marked if intended for casseroling. Joints of loin or haunch can be bought for braising.

HOW MUCH TO BUY

Many cooks find it difficult to judge how much game to buy, especially when it comes to birds as they look so puny. Bear in mind that game is a fairly rich food and therefore portions do not have to be too generous—serve an additional accompaniment if you feel the quantity of meat looks rather mean.

Pigeons: allow one per person.
Partridges: allow one per person.
Pheasant: allow one between two.
Grouse: allow one between two.
Capercaillie: allow one between two.
Rabbit: allow 225 g [½ lb] cut rabbit per person. One average-sized rabbit skinned and jointed by the butcher will serve 4-6.
Hare: hare can only be bought whole. An average-sized hare, skinned and jointed by the butcher will serve 6. Make sure that you get the hare's blood (usually sold in a plastic bag with the hare) for enriching casseroles and jugged hare.
Venison: allow 175 g [6 oz] boneless meat per person. If buying a joint with a bone, allow 225 g [½ lb] meat per person.

OTHER INGREDIENTS

Other ingredients for game casseroles and braises can be divided into marinade, fat, fruit and vegetables, liquid and thickening.

Marinade

All game tends to be dry and this is a tendency which increases as the bird or animal gets older. A marinade helps to break down tough fibres and moisturize the meat. A good marinade consists of an acid element to break down tough fibres and oil to moisturize the meat, plus herbs and spices to add flavour. There are two kinds of marinade for game, cooked and cold.

Cooked marinade: a cooked marinade is used hot and is good for large pieces of venison for braising. The ingredients for the marinade are assembled, brought to the boil and then poured hot on to the meat. Venison marinades always contain juniper berries which have a particular affinity with this meat. Make sure the berries are bruised (do this with a rolling pin or a meat hammer) before adding to the marinade or they will not give up their flavour. A cooked marinade for venison is given in the recipe section.

Cold marinade: for a cold marinade, the ingredients are simply mixed together and then poured over the meat. Once again make sure that spices and berries are crushed so that they will release their flavour. Although cold marinades are less effective than hot marinades they are successful especially if a less gamey flavour is required.

How long to marinade

Game should be marinated for at least four hours. The meat should be turned from time to time so that all sides are coated with the marinade. Most game marinades can be strained and added to the liquid or sauce for the braise or casserole.

Fat

Game must always be sealed in hot fat before you start casseroling or braising. This will seal in the scarce juices. Bacon dripping gives the best flavour. Alternatively, chop about two rashers of streaky bacon and sauté in the bottom of a casserole dish until the fat runs out. This fat can then be used as part of the mirepoix for a braise or in the ingredients for a casserole.

Fruit and vegetables

For braising, game is cooked on a bed of vegetables (and sometimes fruit) called a mirepoix. The classic mirepoix is made from onions, carrots and celery cut into fairly large diced pieces, with the addition of a few parsley stalks, a bay leaf and some thyme. For a game mirepoix fruit such as apples or quince may be included. There should be enough fruit and vegetables to make a good layer up to 5 cm [2"] deep in the bottom of the casserole dish. Some recipes use one vegetable only for the mirepoix (such as partridge with cabbage) and here the same rules apply unless the recipe states differently.

Vegetables are used in game casseroles in exactly the same way as for any other casserole, in that they are served with the meat.

Suitable vegetables to use with game are celery, red or white cabbage, swede, onions, mushrooms, carrots and parsnips. Apples go well with all game birds. Prunes go well with rabbit.

Liquid

The liquid for game casseroles and braises can be a combination of game or chicken stock and alcohol or can have liquid from the marinade added. The only exception where liquid is concerned is when jugged hare is made. Here the blood of the hare is also added.

When using alcohol, use in the proportion of $\frac{1}{4}$ alcohol to $\frac{3}{4}$ stock and marinade mixture if used. You will need about 275 ml [$\frac{1}{2}$ pt] liquid to every 350 g [$\frac{3}{4}$ lb] meat for casseroles and about half this for braises. In braising, the liquid should come about halfway up the sides of the meat.

Thickening

The liquid in game casseroles and braises can be thickened by either tossing the meat in seasoned flour before you fry it, adding a beurre manié to the juices after cooking or adding a velouté of egg and cream to the juices after cooking.

Flour

Always use plain flour and season it with salt and freshly ground black pepper. You will need just enough flour to thinly coat the meat, not to encrust it. During cooking, the flour dissolves into the liquid and thickens it.

Beurre manié

A beurre manié is a combination of two parts butter to one part flour which is mixed to a stiff paste. To thicken an average game casserole you will need a beurre manié made from 15 g [$\frac{1}{2}$ oz] butter and 15 g [$\frac{1}{2}$ oz] flour.

Velouté

A mixture of egg yolks and cream (known as velouté) is a traditional thickening for the liquid from game casseroles and braises. One large egg yolk beaten with 45 ml [3 tablespoons] cream is sufficient for a casserole or braise to serve 4–6.

PREPARING GAME FOR CASSEROLING

Preparation differs slightly for birds and animals.

Birds

Birds are best left whole for both casseroling and braising. They can be portioned afterwards (see step-by-step to portioning). Left whole, the birds retain maximum juice and flavour and the end results are much

better than casseroles where the birds are cut into portions.

The first thing to do when you get your plucked birds home is to see if the butcher has removed the innards. Quite often they are left in and unless you specifically ask, the butcher will not remove them. To remove the innards, enlarge the vent (the hole at the tail end) with a pair of scissors. Make a whole large enough to get your fingers in. Put your fingers inside the bird, grasp the windpipe (the only hard part in the intestines) and pull. All the intestines should come out at once. Separate the liver and windpipe, wash and use for game stock. The rest of the innards can be discarded.

Wash the inside of the bird thoroughly with cold running water. Pick any feathers off the outside and wash the body. The bird is now ready for casseroling or braising.

Rabbit and hare

Rabbit and hare are best bought ready jointed from the butcher. This spares you a great deal of messy preparation.

Venison

Venison is also sold ready to use. Stewing venison or venison chops are ready cut. Haunches for braising are sold whole so no further preparation is necessary.

CASSEROLING AND BRAISING

When you have prepared your game, marinate it, using one of the marinades given in the recipe section. Marinate for at least 4 hours, longer if possible, and turn the game from time to time.

Preparing the stock

While the game is marinating, make stock using the giblets from birds (or, if these are unavailable, chicken livers), a few bruised juniper berries, a scrubbed and halved carrot and a quartered onion. Making giblet stock is described on page 18.

Cooking

Game is braised or casseroled in exactly the same way as meat. The only difference is that cooking times and temperatures will not be exactly the same, so do be sure to follow the times given overleaf. The time and temperature are the same for both braising and casseroling.

Step-by-step to portioning cooked game bird

1 Lift the cooked bird out of the casserole dish. Place on a flat surface.

2 Using kitchen scissors or poultry shears, cut away the backbone and discard.

3 Divide small birds by cutting in half down the breastbone, using a sharp knife.

4 Cut larger birds in half again, cutting at the point where the leg joins the body.

BRAISING AND CASSEROLING TIMES FOR GAME

Oven temperature 180°C [350°F] gas mark 4

Game	Time
Pigeon	1½–2 hours
Partridge	2–2½ hours
Pheasant	2½ hours
Grouse	2½ hours
Capercaillie	2½ hours
Rabbit	2 hours
Hare	2½–3 hours
Venison	2½–3 hours

Portioning birds

After the casserole or braise has been cooked, birds will need to be portioned. Small birds, such as pigeon and partridge and grouse are best halved. Using kitchen scissors or poultry shears, cut away the backbone. Using a sharp knife, cut through the breastbone.

Larger birds can be cut into four portions. Halve as described above then cut in half again, cutting at the point where the leg joins the body. Keep the portions warm in a low oven while you thicken the liquid if necessary, or remove the mirepoix to finish the sauce.

Portioning animals

Animals will not need portioning as the pieces are ready cut. Venison braised in a piece should be sliced thickly and served as suggested (see right).

Reducing the sauce

If you have not tossed the meat in flour to thicken the braising or casseroling juices they will still be quite thin. They can be reduced in three ways.

Before reducing, strain the liquid and reserve the vegetables.

Rapid boiling: return the liquid to the casserole and boil rapidly uncovered until reduced to the desired quantity. Reducing by this method does not really thicken the juices.

Beurre manié: return the juices to the casserole. Set over low heat and add beurre manié a piece at a time, stirring until each piece has dissolved into the liquid. Cook for 2–3 minutes until thick.

Velouté: return the juices to the casserole. Beat together the yolk of a large egg and 45 ml [3 tablespoons] thick cream. Add a little of the hot juice to this mixture and blend. Add the mixture to the liquid in the casserole and cook gently for 2–3 minutes until thickened.

Serving

To serve a game casserole, return the pieces to the sauce if necessary. To serve a braise, arrange the portions or sliced meat on a serving plate. Arrange the reserved mirepoix around it and spoon over some of the hot juice. Serve the rest of the juice separately.

MARINADE FOR VENISON AND HARE

This is a cooked marinade and should be poured on the venison hot. The meat should be marinated for at least 4 hours, overnight if possible. Turn from time to time so that all sides of the meat receive the benefit of the marinade.

MAKES 150 ML [¼ PT]
150 ml [¼ pt] dry red wine
30 ml [2 tablespoons] olive oil
1 small finely chopped onion
2 bay leaves
freshly ground black pepper
4 juniper berries, bruised

1 Combine all the ingredients in a saucepan.

2 Bring to the boil and pour over the meat while hot.

3 When the meat has been removed, the marinade can be strained and added to the cooking liquid or boiled down to add to the finished casserole.

MARINADE FOR RABBIT AND BIRDS

Pour the marinade over the meat while it is still hot. Leave for at least 4 hours, turning the meat occasionally.

MAKES 150 ML [¼ PT]
1 large onion, skinned and chopped
150 ml [¼ pt] brandy or medium sherry
5 ml [1 teaspoon] powdered thyme
1 bay leaf
4 chopped parsley stalks
30 ml [2 tablespoons] olive oil
4 bruised allspice berries

1 Combine all the ingredients. Pour over the meat. Turn from time to time.

2 If wished, the marinade may be strained and added to the cooking liquid for the braise or casserole.

Marinating game birds helps to tenderize their rather tough flesh and also prevents drying out when the birds are cooked.

PIGEONS WITH CHERRIES

You can use either fresh or canned cherries for this dish. *Feuillitons*, which are little squares of puff pastry, are traditional accompaniments to this dish. Marinate the pigeons in the marinade for birds given on page 71. Serve the pigeon with game chips and a green vegetable such as broccoli.

SERVES 4
4 pigeons
150 ml [¼ pt] marinade
50 g [2 oz] bacon dripping
2 shallots or large spring onions
25 g [1 oz] flour
550 ml [1 pt] game or chicken stock
bouquet garni

30 ml [2 tablespoons] soured cream
225 g [½ lb] stoned red cherries
25 g [1 oz] butter

1 Marinate the pigeons for 4 hours.

2 Heat the oven to 180°C [350°F] gas mark 4. Heat the bacon dripping in a large heavy-based casserole.

3 Brown the pigeons in the bacon dripping until all sides are sealed. Lift out.

4 Skin and chop the shallots or spring onions. Sauté in the bacon fat.

5 Stir in the flour. Cook for 2 minutes until just turning brown.

6 Return the pigeons to the dish. Pour on the stock and any strained left-over marinade. Add the bouquet garni.

7 Cook in the centre of the oven for about 1½ hours.

8 Remove the pigeons from the casserole and cut in half. Strain the sauce into a clean pan.

9 Set the sauce over low heat and allow to boil and reduce by about half.

10 While the sauce is reducing, melt the butter in a heavy-based frying-pan over low heat. Add the cherries and sauté for 3 minutes.

11 Stir the soured cream into the reduced sauce. Return the pigeons to the sauce to reheat.

12 Scatter the cherries over the meat before serving.

CASSEROLED PHEASANT WITH CELERY AND CREAM

Here is an example of how game casseroles can be thickened with egg yolk and cream. This is one of the best ways to serve a pheasant which is past its youth and is a method which can also be used with chicken, turkey, grouse and capercaillie. Marinate the birds using the marinade for pheasant given on page 71.

SERVES 4
2 pheasants
150 ml [¼ pt] marinade
75 g [3 oz] bacon dripping
2 rashers middle cut bacon
250 ml [½ pt] game or chicken stock
bouquet garni
125 ml [4 fl oz] port
2 celery hearts
150 ml [¼ pt] thick cream
1 large egg yolk
salt and black pepper

1 Prepare and marinate the birds for at least 4 hours or overnight.

2 Melt the bacon dripping in a heavy-based casserole over low heat. Heat the oven to 180°C [350°F] gas mark 4.

3 Brown the birds in the fat, turning so that all sides are coloured.

4 Remove the rind from the bacon rashers and cut the bacon into strips. Remove the pheasants from the casserole.

5 Lightly fry the bacon strips. Return the pheasants to the casserole. Add the stock, port, bouquet garni. Place in the oven.

6 Cut the celery hearts into rounds. Add to the pheasant when it has been in the oven about 30 minutes.

7 Continue cooking for a further 2 hours or until the bird is tender.

8 Lift the birds and celery rounds out of the casserole. Cut birds into portions and arrange on a warmed serving dish. Keep warm.

9 Beat the egg yolk and cream together. Add a little of the hot liquid from the casserole dish.

10 Set the casserole dish over low heat. Gradually add all the egg and cream, stirring all the time. Heat gently but do not boil or the sauce will curdle. Season if necessary.

11 Spoon the sauce over the birds.

PARTRIDGE EN COCOTTE NORMANDE

End of season partridges become tender and delicious if braised with apples and cider. Pigeons can also be used for this recipe. Make sure that the cider is dry. Sweet cider will spoil the flavour of the partridges. This recipe is particularly suitable for partridges which have been hung until they are very gamey. Use the marinade for game birds given on page 71.

SERVES 2
2 partridges
150 ml [¼ pt] marinade
2 rashers streaky bacon
1 medium-sized onion
1 cooking apple

150 ml [¼ pt] dry cider
150 ml [¼ pt] game stock
bouquet garni
salt and black pepper

For the garnish:
2 cooking apples
25 g [1 oz] butter
fresh parsley sprigs

1 Wash the partridges inside and out and remove any feathers. Marinate for 4 hours or overnight. Heat the oven to 180°C [350°F] gas mark 4.

2 Cut the rind off the bacon. Cut the bacon into strips. Place in the casserole over low heat.

3 Cook the bacon until the fat is running freely. Add the partridges and brown well on all sides. Remove from the dish and set aside.

4 Skin and chop the onion and add to the fat. Peel and chop the apple and add to the fat. Cook over low heat for about 3 minutes, turning from time to time.

5 Return the partridges to the dish. Add the cider, stock, strained marinade and bouquet garni.

6 Place in the oven and cook for 2–2½ hours, covered until the partridges are tender when pierced with a skewer.

7 Just before the partridges are ready, peel, core and slice the apples. Melt the butter in a heavy-based frying-pan over low heat and fry the apple rings until golden on both sides. Set aside.

8 Remove the partridges from the casserole. Cut away the backbone using kitchen scissors or poultry shears then halve the birds. Place on a serving dish. Arrange the apple rings on the dish and place in a low oven or warming drawer.

9 Strain the liquid. Return strained liquid to the casserole and boil rapidly for about 4 minutes until reduced. Check seasoning.

10 Spoon a little of the hot sauce over the meat and serve the remainder separately. Garnish with parsley just before serving.

RABBIT WITH PRUNES

⬙⬙⬙ *Preparation for this dish must begin a day in advance as it is essential that the rabbit is marinated overnight. Use the marinade given for birds and rabbit on page 71.*

SERVES 4
1 rabbit, skinned and jointed
150 ml [¼ pt] marinade
225 g [½ lb] prunes
575 ml [1 pt] strained tea
50 g [2 oz] bacon dripping
15 g [½ oz] flour
150 ml [¼ pt] dry red wine
250 ml [½ pt] game or chicken stock
salt and black pepper

1 Marinate the rabbit and soak the prunes in the tea for 8 hours.

2 Lift the rabbit pieces out of the marinade. Pat dry. Heat the oven to 180°C [350°F] gas mark 4.

3 Gently melt the bacon dripping in a heavy-based casserole over low heat. Add the rabbit pieces and brown on all sides. Remove.

4 Sprinkle the flour into the casserole and allow to brown. Add the wine and stock.

5 Replace the rabbit. Add the prunes and any remaining soaking liquid.

6 Cover and cook in the centre of the oven for about 2 hours.

7 If there is more than 275 ml [½ pt] liquid remaining at the end of cooking, lift out the rabbit pieces, strain out prunes and reduce the sauce by rapid boiling. Check seasoning. Return rabbit pieces and prunes before serving.

RABBIT WITH LENTIL PUREE

⬙⬙⬙ *Lentils and rabbit make a delicious combination, especially as the pulses are cooked with the rabbit, giving a delicious flavour. Start preparations the day before.*

SERVES 4
1 rabbit, skinned and jointed
150 ml [¼ pt] marinade
100 g [¼ lb] lentils
1 small onion
1 celery stick
bouquet garni
75 g [3 oz] butter
4 slices white bread

1 Marinate the rabbit for at least 8 hours. Pat the pieces dry. Soak the lentils, overnight, in enough water to cover.

2 Put the rabbit in a large casserole or stewpan with the lentils and any remaining soaking water.

3 Skin and chop the onion. Scrub and chop the celery and add to the pan. Add bouquet garni.

4 Add enough water just to cover. Cover the pan or casserole and simmer over low heat for 2½ hours until the rabbit and lentils are tender.

5 Lift the rabbit out of the liquid and keep warm.

6 Strain out the vegetables and

lentils. Rub through a sieve to purée. Put the purée in a clean pan.

7 Add enough of the rabbit cooking liquid to make the purée a coating consistency. Stir in 25 g [1 oz] butter, season to taste.

8 Return the rabbit to the pan and allow to reheat gently.

9 While the rabbit is reheating, melt the butter in a heavy-based saucepan over low heat. Cut the crusts off the bread and cut each slice into four triangles.

10 Fry the bread until golden on both sides. Serve the rabbit surrounded by croûtons.

GROUSE WITH CABBAGE

Partridge is the classic favourite for this dish but grouse actually tastes much better. Use a firm, hearty green cabbage—not the white kind, it does not have such a good flavour and the finished dish will not look particularly attractive. Marinate the birds using the marinade given on page 71.

SERVES 4
2 grouse
150 ml [¼ pt] marinade
2 medium-sized onions
2 medium-sized carrots
1 medium-sized cabbage
175 g [6 oz] streaky bacon
** in one piece**
25 g [1 oz] bacon dripping
100 g [¼ lb] good pork
** sausages**
bouquet garni
250 ml [½ pt] game or chicken
** stock**
salt
freshly ground black pepper
freshly chopped parsley to
** garnish**

1 Prepare the grouse and marinate for at least 4 hours using the marinade for birds given on page 71.

2 Skin and chop the onions. Scrub and dice the carrots. Trim the cabbage, cut into four, remove centre stalk and wash.

3 Blanch the bacon and cabbage in boiling salted water for about six minutes. Meanwhile heat the oven

to 180°C [350°F] gas mark 4.

4 Place the dripping in a large, heavy-based casserole. Pat the grouse dry and brown on all sides.

5 Take the grouse out of the dish. Add the carrots and onion and brown. Drain the cabbage, cut each quarter in half.

6 Cut the rind off the bacon. Cut the flesh into strips.

7 Remove the onion and carrot from the dish. Add the sausages and brown lightly. Remove.

8 Lay half the cabbage on the bottom of the dish. Place the birds on top of the cabbage, add the sausages and bacon.

9 Place remaining cabbage and other vegetables on top of the birds.

10 Add the stock and seasonings. Cover and cook in the centre of the oven for 2–2½ hours.

11 To serve, remove the birds. Halve. Place on a warmed serving dish.

12 Remove the sauages and slice. Arrange around the birds with the bacon strips and vegetables.

13 Pour a little of the liquid over the dish. Serve remainder separately. Sprinkle the grouse with chopped parsley just before serving.

BRAISED VENISON

If you are in doubt about the origin or age of your venison, marinate it well and braise it. Its own good flavour enriched by the marinade needs no extras. Use the cooked marinade given on page 71, and marinate for at least 24 hours for maximum flavour.

SERVES 6
1.4 kg [3 lb] haunch or leg
** of venison**
150 ml [¼ pt] marinade
2 medium-sized onions
2 medium-sized carrots
2 sticks celery
1 small turnip
25 g [1 oz] bacon dripping
bouquet garni
275 ml [½ pt] good game or

beef stock
salt
freshly ground black pepper
15 ml [1 tablespoon]
** redcurrant jelly**
15 g [½ oz] butter
15 g [½ oz] plain flour

1 Cut any membranes, gristle and ragged ends off the meat, and any fat. Marinate the joint for 24 hours. Turn it over several times.

2 Skin and chop the onions. Scrub and chop carrots and celery. Peel and chop turnip. Wipe and dry the meat. Heat the oven to 180°C [350°F] gas mark 4.

3 Heat the dripping in a large stewpan or flameproof casserole with a lid. Put in the meat. Brown it on all sides. Take it out.

4 Put the mirepoix into the same fat in the pan. Lower the heat. Cover the pan, and cook the mirepoix very gently for 6–7 minutes. Shake the pan from time to time to make sure that the vegetables do not stick to the bottom.

5 Uncover the pan, and put in the venison. Add the bouquet garni and the stock.

6 Cover and place in the centre of the oven. Cook for 2½–3 hours or until the meat is tender.

7 When tender, lift the meat with a carving fork. Hold it over the pan to let the juices drip off. Put it on a heated serving dish. Strain out the vegetables and arrange around the meat. Keep hot.

8 Skim excess fat off the braising liquid. Add the redcurrant jelly. Over moderate heat, stir the sauce until the jelly dissolves. Take the pan off the heat.

9 Mix the butter and flour together to a smooth paste. Stir it into the sauce in small pieces.

10 Return the pan to the heat, and stir until it boils and thickens to the consistency of thin cream. Check the seasoning.

11 Spoon a little of the sauce over the venison. Serve the rest in a heated sauce-boat, with the meat.

JUGGED HARE

This traditional English recipe is very rich indeed. Buy the hare ready skinned and jointed from the butcher. He will give you the blood which is used in the casserole in a plastic bag. Do not buy the hare until the day before you plan to serve the casserole as the meat can dry out very quickly. Marinate the hare using the hare and venison marinade given on page 71.

SERVES 6
1 large hare, jointed
150 ml [¼ pt] marinade
15 ml [1 tablespoon] bacon
 dripping
2 large onions
2 cloves
5 black peppercorns
1 celery stick
1 carrot
5 ml [1 teaspoon] bruised
 allspice berries
bouquet garni
pinch of salt
juice of 1 lemon
strip of lemon rind
850 ml [1½ pt] game stock
15 g [½ oz] butter
15 g [½ oz] plain flour
blood of the hare
150 ml [¼ pt] port
15 ml [1 tablespoon] redcurrant
 jelly
8 shallots
100 g [¼ lb] mushrooms

1 Marinate the hare for 4 hours or overnight, turning occasionally.

2 Pat the pieces dry. Melt the bacon fat in a large casserole over low heat. Add the hare pieces and fry until sealed on all sides. Heat the oven to 180°C [350°F] gas mark 4.

3 Remove from heat. Skin the onions and stick a clove into each one. Add to the casserole. Add peppercorns.

4 Scrub and chop the celery stick. Scrub and quarter the carrot. Add to the casserole.

5 Add remaining spices, lemon juice and rind. Pour in the stock.

6 Cover, place in the centre of the oven and cook for about 3 hours.

7 Set aside the hare. Strain the juices. Discard the vegetables. Trim the shallots and wipe the mushrooms. Brown shallots lightly in a pan and add mushrooms.

8 Combine the butter and flour to make a beurre manié. Set the gravy over low heat. Add the beurre manié a little at a time. The liquid should be thickened to the consistency of thin cream. Add shallots and mushrooms.

9 Allow the liquid to boil then remove from the heat. Add about 45 ml [3 tablespoons] of the gravy to the blood of the hare, stirring after each addition.

10 Gradually add the blood to the gravy, stirring well. Stir in the port and redcurrant jelly.

11 Place the hare pieces in a clean flameproof dish. Pour over the gravy. Reheat carefully, shaking from time to time. Do not stir as this may break up the pieces of hare.

A perfect setting

A galantine provides the perfect centrepiece for a cold table. It is an elegant dish which demands some careful preparation but no last minute attention. Being completely boneless and firmly rolled means that it is particularly easy to carve. It is versatile, too, in that it can be served with hot vegetables or with a salad and bread, as befits the occasion.

A galantine is a very clever way of extending meat that is to be served cold and making it more interesting. The idea has been around for a long time. Originally, only poultry was used but then other types of bird and eventually cuts of meat were turned into galantines. Nowadays, recipes can be found for chicken, turkey, game birds, veal, pork and beef galantines. The making of a galantine is a rather long and involved process but equally it is a decorative and rewarding skill to learn.

A galantine is a boned roll of uncooked meat, stuffed with a well-flavoured and substantial stuffing, poached in stock, cooled and finally coated with aspic or chaudfroid or a layer of each. The process sounds more complicated than it in fact is, but this is certainly not a quick dish to prepare. It is very sensible, and essential if using a turkey, to cook the galantine at least the day before it is needed so that it can cool at room temperature overnight. Once it is cold the bird can be stored in the refrigerator in its muslin wrappings until needed, but not for more than 2-3 days.

A galantine is an ideal dish for a summer party, especially if you have an awkward number to serve, such as five or seven. The stuffing can be relied upon to make a bird that, plain roasted, would serve four or six, stretch to serve the extra one with absolutely no difficulty. It is also a good dish for a party in that it is prepared in advance by necessity and there is no last minute preparation.

If the weather suddenly changes and you do not want to serve a completely cold meal, hot vegetables go with a galantine just as well as a salad. No accompanying sauce is needed as this is already coating the meat, in jellied form. The lack of bones and the shape and firm texture of the roll make it easy to carve, and no one can criticize its appearance. A delicate garnish of fresh fruit or vegetables is all that is needed to decorate the galantine and this again is arranged in advance.

INGREDIENTS

There are three principal ingredients in a poultry galantine: the bird, the stuffing and the coating. You will also need a quantity of stock in which to poach the bird, made from the carcass and giblets, and various fruit and vegetables to garnish the final result.

The bird

If you are serving a large number of people your first choice will obviously be a turkey. Once sliced a galantine will dry out, so calculate carefully the size of turkey required for the number of guests. If you are serving a smaller number you can choose between a chicken, a duck and a game bird.

A galantine is one dish where a frozen bird can be used very successfully. The stuffing adds plenty of flavour and, as the galantine is poached, there is no danger of the flesh becoming dry. This is also an excellent method for cooking birds which may no longer be in their prime. The cooking can be extended for an older and tougher bird to ensure tender results.

Frozen birds are always sold oven-ready with the giblets inside. Thaw the bird in the refrigerator in its wrappings for the calculated time (see on page 5). When completely thawed, remove and reserve the gib-

lets and rinse the bird inside with cold water.

The stuffing

The stuffing for a galantine is always substantial. It usually contains a large quantity of minced meat, seasoned and flavoured with herbs and a little onion, and moistened with a well-flavoured liquor such as Madeira, cognac or sherry.

The stuffing must be moist as meat that is left to become cold is usually drier than when it is hot. For this reason, pork or pork sausage meat is included. Veal is also used in quantity as the flavour is mild, and smaller quantities of ham or bacon are used for flavouring but not so that they overpower the flavour of the bird. The ham or other flavouring meat can be cut into strips and layered between two quantities of stuffing. This will give a decorative effect to the cooked galantine when it is sliced. Many variations can be added to the basic stuffing mixture.

The coating

A galantine can be coated with aspic alone, with a chaudfroid sauce alone or with a glazing of aspic over the sauce.

Aspic is a smooth, shimmering clear jelly made from consommé. It sets over the galantine to form a transparent, lightly coloured glaze. Consommé is made from the stock in which the bird is poached, and the consommé is then used to make the aspic. The stock for the consommé must be clarified with the white and shell of an egg. If it does not set when cold, some gelatine can be used. You will need 25 g [1 oz] of gelatine for every 575 ml [1 pt] of stock used. Aspic is also obtainable in powdered form.

Chaudfroid is a thick, flavoursome sauce which is jellied with a small quantity of aspic and when poured over the food sets to form a moist opaque coating. Both chaudfroid and aspic set firmly enough to be sliced with the meat.

The bird must be completely cold before it is coated and the aspic or chaudfroid is used while still unset but cool. If the chicken or the sauce were warm, the coating would not set. If you wish to use a combination of both coatings, a glazing of aspic can be added after the chaudfroid coating has been allowed to set firmly.

The garnish

A simple, fresh fruit or vegetable garnish is used to decorate the top of a galantine. There is a variety of pieces of fruit and vegetables that can be used and they should be chosen for their decorative qualities rather than their flavour. Strips and thin slices are best as they can be firmly secured to the bird. Larger pieces would be less secure and could make carving a little difficult. Strips of citrus peel, anchovies, cucumber, sliced radishes, cloves, capers, sliced gherkins, sliced olives and thin slices of celery are some of the garnishes that can be used to decorate a galantine.

If the coating is aspic alone, the garnish can be arranged by being dipped into the aspic and stuck on the galantine. When secure, the aspic coating can be poured over. With a chaudfroid coating, the garnish is arranged in the coating before it has been allowed to set and the two set together. Aspic shapes can be used here.

When using as aspic glaze over a chaudfroid coating, the cool aspic is poured over when the chaudfroid and the garnish are firmly set.

QUANTITIES

Galantines are a good way of stretching a single bird to serve a larger number of people. The stuffing is substantial as it is usually meat-based. This, combined with a boneless bird, means portions do not have to be too large.

Bear in mind that the larger the bird, the higher the proportion of meat to bone—small birds weighing up to 2.2 kg [5 lb] give about half this weight of meat when boned: larger, heavier birds yield meat in an increased ratio. However, birds over 4.5 kg [10 lb] are not really suitable. By the time they are stuffed, they will be so large as to make handling difficult. It will also be difficult to cook the bird through to the centre, and you probably will not have a pan large enough to take the galantine.

The weight of the stuffing used can be as much as half the weight of the boned meat, depending on the number of servings required. For example, a 2.2 kg [5 lb] chicken boned will yield about 1.1 kg [2½ lb] meat. This can be combined with up to 600 g [1¼ lb] stuffing: allowing 175 g [6 oz] per person, this will serve about 10.

METHOD

Making a galantine is rather a long and involved process though it can be effectively divided into several clear stages. You should allow at least six hours for boning, making the stock and cooking the galantine. The bird must then be allowed to cool at room temperature which, for a turkey, definitely means overnight. The final stage is the coating, which must be allowed to set firmly (2 hours in the refrigerator) before the galantine can be served.

Boning the bird

The first step in preparing a galantine is to bone out the bird so that you are left with the skin and flesh in one piece. This is not as difficult as it may sound but the first few attempts will undoubtedly be time-consuming. Detailed, step-by-step instructions are given here for boning a chicken. Always use a sharp knife and keep the bones and trimmings for stock.

A turkey, duck or game bird is boned in a similar way. The size and weight of a large turkey will make it more difficult to handle and for the same reason, small game birds will be more fiddly. The most important thing to remember is not to pierce or tear the skin during the process. If the skin remains whole, there will be no danger of the stuffing seeping out when the galantine is cooking.

When the bird is boned, cover it lightly and store it in the refrigerator until you are ready to stuff it.

Making the stock and stuffing

Once the bird is boned, the carcass and other bones are used with the giblets to make a well-flavoured stock.

The stock required will take quite some time to cook as the flavours from the bones, giblets and vegetables must be given up to the liquid. When it is cooked, the stock should be strained and degreased ready for use.

While the stock is simmering, and in order to save time, the stuffing can be prepared. Trim any skin and bone from the meat and mince the meat finely. If an onion is used, peel, chop and mince this as well. Mix the stuffing ingredients and keep in a bowl covered with a piece of damp greaseproof paper until you are ready to stuff the bird. Any stuffing ingredients that are to be used in layers can be sliced ready for use.

Step-by-step to boning a chicken

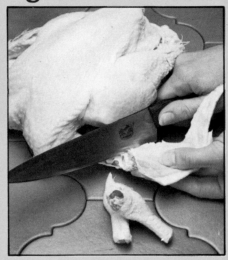

1 Remove the giblets and wipe the bird inside and out. Gently pull out any bits of feather.

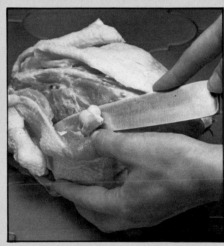

2 Lay the chicken on its back. Cut off the legs at the first joint and the wings at the second.

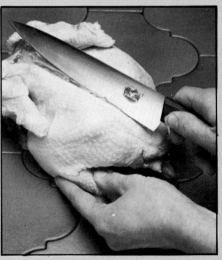

3 Turn the chicken on to its breast. Using a very sharp knife, make a cut along the backbone.

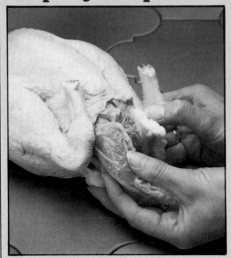

4 Work the skin and flesh away on both sides, holding the knife flat against the carcass.

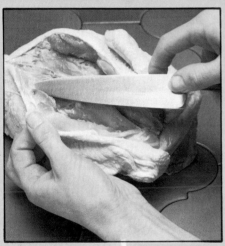

5 When you reach the legs, sever each thigh bone from the carcass and work the thigh flesh loose.

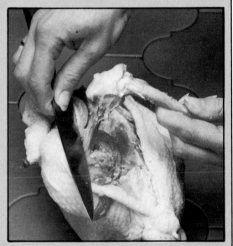

6 Holding the drumstick, loosen the flesh as far as the thigh. Draw out the complete leg bone.

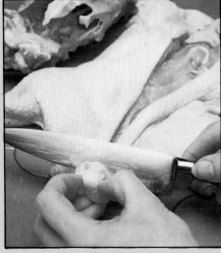

7 Loosen the flesh up each wing to the body. Sever wing bone from carcass and draw out the bone.

8 Work the flesh away from the ribs being careful not to cut the skin. Lift out the carcass.

9 Lay the chicken flat, skin down. Cut off the parson's nose. Turn the legs and wings inside out.

Step-by-step to chicken galantine

SERVES 6-8
**1 oven-ready chicken weighing
    1.4 kg [3 lb]**
salt
freshly ground black pepper

For the stock:
700 g [1½ lb] knuckle of veal,
    chopped and blanched
2 large carrots, quartered
2 Spanish onions, quartered
1 leek, sliced
1 celery stick, sliced
bouquet garni
6 white peppercorns

For the stuffing:
100 g [¼ lb] stewing veal
100 g [¼ lb] gammon
100 g [¼ lb] sausage meat

50 g [2 oz] fresh white
    breadcrumbs
30 ml [2 tablespoons] lemon
    juice
zest of half a lemon
large pinch of nutmeg
1 small egg

For the coating:
25 g [1 oz] gelatine
    (optional)
7 black olives
strips of cucumber skin

1 Bone the chicken following the step-by-step instructions. Cover the chicken and refrigerate.

5 Season the stuffing mixture generously and add the spice. Beat the egg, add and mix well.

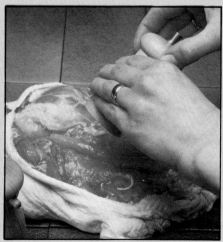

6 Spread the boned chicken out flat on a board, skin down. Season the flesh with salt and pepper.

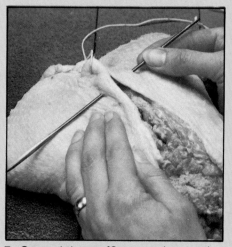

7 Spread the stuffing evenly over the centre of the chicken. Draw together into a roll and sew up.

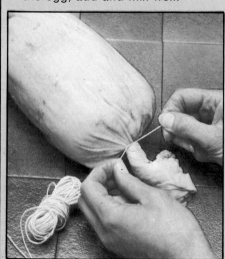

11 When cool enough to handle, either tighten the muslin wrappings or renew and tie tightly.

12 Put the galantine between two plates and put a weight on top. Leave to become quite cold.

13 Remove muslin wrappings and cut away trussing. Put gelantine on cake rack with plate underneath.

80

2 Make the stock using the bones and giblets from the chicken and other stock ingredients.

3 While the stock is simmering, prepare the stuffing. Mince the veal, chop and mince the gammon.

4 Mix the minced meat with the sausage meat and breadcrumbs. Add the lemon juice and zest.

8 Wrap the galantine in a double layer of muslin and tie the ends together to make a tight roll.

9 Pour the strained stock into a saucepan. Immerse the galantine. Cover and simmer for 1½ hours.

10 When cooked, drain the galantine over the pan and set aside to cool slightly. Reserve the stock.

14 Make 575 ml [1 pt] aspic using some of the stock. Use gelatine if necessary. Leave to cool.

15 Halve and stone olives. Dip pieces of garnish into the aspic. Stick in place. Allow to set.

16 Pour the aspic along the top of the galantine and let it run down to completely coat the bird.

Stuffing and cooking the bird

Take the bird from the refrigerator and spread it out flat on a board, skin down. Season the cut surface with salt and pepper. Spread the stuffing evenly down the centre of the bird. Arrange any solid ingredients you may have, such as strips of ham and tongue or pieces of olives, etc between two layers of stuffing.

Thread a trussing needle with some fine string or strong cotton thread. Draw the edges of the bird together and stitch securely to form a roll. Wrap the roll in a double layer of muslin and tie the ends firmly.

Strain the prepared stock into a saucepan just large enough to hold the galantine. Immerse the galantine in the stock: it must be completely covered. Cover the saucepan securely and simmer the galantine for the time given in the recipe.

Cooling and pressing the galantine

Drain the cooked galantine over the pan for a few moments and then set it aside. Reserve the stock. When the galantine is cool enough to handle, either tighten the muslin wrappings or change them for clean ones and tie these tightly round the roll. Put the galantine between two plates and put a weight on top. Leave the galantine to cool at room temperature until it is quite cold. This may mean overnight depending on the size of the galantine.

At this stage the galantine can be stored in the refrigerator, in its muslin wrappings, until it is needed. It should not be stored for longer than 2-3 days.

Coating the galantine

Depending on the chosen coating, make a quantity of aspic and/or chaudfroid. For a medium chicken you will need about 575 ml [1 pt] of either sauce. The reserved poultry stock is used in the making of the aspic sauce, and it may not, in fact, require any additional setting agent.

Take the galantine from the refrigerator and take off the wrappings. Undo the trussing stitches. Put the bird on a rack and slip a plate underneath. If using chaudfroid, pour over an even coating of sauce, arrange the garnish and allow to set in the refrigerator for 2 hours. If using aspic, set the garnish in place with a dab of aspic and when firm apply an even glaze of aspic. Leave to set in

the refrigerator for 2 hours.

If wished, an aspic glaze can be applied over the chaudfroid coating once it has set firmly.

Alternatively, slice the cold, ungarnished galantine and arrange on a serving dish. Apply an even coating of aspic over the slices and leave in the refrigerator to set.

SERVING A GALANTINE

A whole galantine makes a marvellous centrepiece for a cold table and can be carved very easily after your guests are assembled. In this case it simply needs to be arranged on a serving dish with a plain garnish of lettuce, chopped aspic, watercress and other salad vegetables. You may wish to do the carving before the guests arrive so that you can forget the food and concentrate on them. In this case, the galantine can be coated and garnished in the normal way and sliced just before serving. Arrange the slices on a serving dish, garnish and serve fairly promptly.

The alternative is to serve aspic-glazed slices of galantine. Once the aspic has set a simple garnish can be arranged to suit the size and shape of the dish. This is a very practical idea if the slicing has to be done in advance, for example, for a wedding reception, as it keeps the meat moist very effectively.

GALANTINE OF PHEASANT

◪◪◪ *This is an excellent way in which to serve a pheasant if you have any doubts about its tenderness and do not want to casserole it. With a veal and ham stuffing, one pheasant will serve four with no difficulty. The galantine can be served whole but in this recipe the serving suggestion involves slicing the galantine and then coating the slices with aspic.*

You will need 1.15 L [2 pt] previously made brown stock (homemade), in order to make a well-flavoured game stock. The other ingredients and directions for making the stock are given on page 18. Add the brown stock to the giblet stock with 700 g [1½ lb] game carcasses. If the clarified stock does not set firmly enough when cold, use 25 g [1 oz] gelatine.

SERVES 4
**1 pheasant weighing about
   1.15 kg [2½ lb]
salt**

**freshly ground black pepper
850 ml [1½ pt] game stock**

**For the stuffing:
100 g [¼ lb] stewing veal
175 g [6 oz] ham
25 g [1 oz] fresh white
   breadcrumbs
1 small onion
10 ml [2 teaspoons] freshly
   chopped sage
15 ml [1 tablespoon] freshly
   chopped parsley
salt
freshly ground black pepper
45 ml [3 tablespoons] Madeira**

**For the garnish:
½ orange, peeled and sliced
fresh watercress sprigs**

1 Wipe the bird inside and out with a damp cloth. Bone the bird, following the step-by-step instructions.

2 Use the bones, giblets and carcasses to make the game stock as detailed on page 18.

3 While the stock is simmering, make the stuffing. Mince the veal and ham finely and mix with the breadcrumbs.

4 Peel, chop and mince the onion and add to the meat and breadcrumbs.

5 Add the herbs, season well with salt and pepper and pour in the Madeira. Mix well and check and adjust the flavour if necessary with a little more herbs and salt.

6 Spread the pheasant out on a flat surface, skin down. Season with salt and pepper. Spoon the stuffing mixture on to it and spread in evenly down the centre with the back of a spoon.

7 Draw the edges of the bird together to form a roll. Sew the edges together securely using strong cotton thread or fine string and a trussing needle.

8 Wrap the galantine in a double layer of muslin, tying the ends to make a neat shape.

9 Place the galantine in a pan just large enough to hold it. Pour over sufficient strained stock to cover. Cover the pan.

10 Set over a low heat and bring to simmering point. Simmer the galantine for 1 hour.

11 Remove the galantine, holding it over the pan to drain. Set it aside until it is cool enough to handle. Reserve the stock.

12 Either tighten the muslin wrapping or change them for clean ones. Then press the galantine between two plates, with a weight on top, until it is quite cold.

13 Store the galantine in its muslin wrappings, lightly covered, in the refrigerator if not needed immediately.

14 When ready to decorate, make 425 ml [¾ pt] aspic using the cold stock and some gelatine if necessary.

15 Unwrap the galantine and remove the trussing stitches. Using a sharp knife, carve the galantine in even slices and arrange these on a serving dish.

16 The aspic should be cool but not set. Using a spoon, pour the aspic over the slices, coating them generously. Transfer the dish to the refrigerator and leave to set for 2 hours.

17 When ready to serve, arrange the orange slices and watercress sprigs at one end of the dish or around the glazed slices, according to the size and shape of your dish. The rind can be left on the orange for extra colour.

CHICKEN GALANTINE EN CHAUDFROID

◼◼◼ *This recipe combines the use of chaudfroid sauce and aspic. Fresh tomatoes are added to the chicken stock to give the aspic a bold colour. The chaudfroid is based on a velouté sauce which is much richer, both in colour and texture than a béchamel sauce. A béchamel sauce could be used, if preferred, and the aspic coating could be omitted if you suddenly run short of time. Use home-made chicken stock if possible.*

SERVES 6–8
1 oven-ready chicken weighing 1.5 kg [3½ lb]
salt
freshly ground black pepper
1.15 L [2 pt] chicken stock
700 g [1½ lb] ripe tomatoes
150 ml [¼ pt] dry white wine

For the stuffing:
175 g [6 oz] lean veal
175 g [6 oz] lean pork
1 Spanish onion
100 g [¼ lb] fried mushrooms, cold
50 g [2 oz] fresh white breadcrumbs
30 ml [2 tablespoons] freshly chopped parsley
30 ml [2 tablespoons] drained capers
salt and pepper
large pinch of cayenne
large pinch of mace
50 ml [2 fl oz] dry sherry
1 large egg

For the coating:
400 ml [¾ pt] velouté sauce
5 ml [1 teaspoon] gelatine

For the garnish:
radish slices
cucumber skin and slices
orange peel and slices
cloves

1 Bone the chicken following the step-by-step instructions. Cover lightly and refrigerate until needed.

2 Make the stock following the instructions on page 18, and using the chicken bones and giblets.

3 While the stock is simmering, make the stuffing. Chop and mince the veal and pork. Peel, chop and mince the onion.

4 Put the minced meat and onion in a bowl with the cold cooked mushrooms and breadcrumbs. Add the parsley and chop and add the capers. Season well with salt and pepper and add the spices.

5 Pour in the sherry. Beat the egg lightly, add to the mixture and beat together well.

6 Season, stuff, roll and wrap the chicken as shown in the step-by-step instructions.

7 Roughly chop the tomatoes and put into a saucepan large enough to hold the galantine. Add wine.

8 Place the galantine in the pan. Pour over enough strained stock to cover the galantine. Cover the pan and simmer for 1½ hours. Drain the cooked galantine over the pan and set aside to cool. Reserve the stock.

9 When cool enough to handle, press the galantine as shown in the step-by-step instructions.

10 Make 700 ml [1¼ pt] aspic with the reserved stock, using a recipe or powdered aspic.

11 Make the chaudfroid sauce using the velouté sauce, 150 ml [¼ pt] aspic and the gelatine. Set the sauce aside and allow it to cool. When it will coat the back of a wooden spoon, the sauce is ready.

12 Set the chicken galantine on a cake rack with a plate underneath. Coat the chicken with the sauce, pouring it along the centre and allowing it to run down to completely coat the galantine.

13 Arrange the garnish in the sauce, making a pretty design.

14 Transfer the galantine, still on the

10 ml [2 teaspoons] freshly
   chopped sage
salt
50 ml [2 fl oz] brandy or sherry
1 medium-sized egg

1 Chop the veal, pork and ham and mince finely. Put into a large bowl with the breadcrumbs.

2 Peel, chop and mince the onion and add to the bowl.

3 Season the mixture generously with pepper and mix in the fresh herbs. Add salt to taste.

4 Pour in the liquor. Beat the egg lightly and add to the bowl. Mix the stuffing mixture very well. Cover with damp greaseproof paper until required.

Variations

● For a spicy stuffing, omit the herbs and add a pinch of nutmeg, a pinch of allspice, 30 ml [2 tablespoons] lemon juice and the zest of half a lemon.

● To make a sausage meat stuffing, replace the pork with sausage meat. Use with chicken, capon or turkey.

● For poultry stuffing for game birds replace the veal with the same quantity of chicken meat, marinated for 2 hours in 30 ml [2 tablespoons] Madeira and 30 ml [2 tablespoons] brandy. Use thyme instead of sage and omit the cognac or sherry, using the marinating liquor instead.

● Add 50 g [2 oz] coarsely chopped pistachio nuts and 25 g [1 oz] sliced stuffed green olives to the spicy stuffing variation above.

● A chequerboard effect is made by omitting the ham from the herbed stuffing mixture. Using 175 g [6 oz] ham and 100 g [¼ lb] cooked tongue, slice the meat and cut it into strips about 1.25 cm [½"] wide. Layer these, with 15 ml [1 tablespoon] drained capers and thin strips of pimento, between two layers of stuffing.

● To make a mushroom stuffing, add 100 g [¼ lb] fried mushrooms and 6 chopped black olives to the herbed stuffing mixture and omit the breadcrumbs.

● To make an orange-flavoured stuffing, use 30 ml [2 tablespoons] orange juice, and the zest of an orange. Use brandy rather than sherry.

● For a fruity stuffing, add 100 g [¼ lb] chopped dates, the pulped flesh of an orange and 50 g [2 oz] chopped walnuts to the orange stuffing.

rack, to the refrigerator to set for 2 hours.

15 When the chaudfroid coating is thoroughly set, bring the galantine out of the refrigerator. If the aspic has set firmly, warm it gently to melt it slightly and pour it over the coated galantine. Return to the refrigerator for a further 2 hours.

16 Serve the galantine on a large dish, from which it can be sliced.

Variation

● If you do not have time to apply an aspic coating and allow it to set, when you have made it turn into a baking tray to set while the chaudfroid coating is setting on the galantine. Serve the galantine in the chaudfroid sauce, garnished with bits of orange peel and radish and spoon the cold aspic around the galantine. Serve with a selection of salads.

HERBED STUFFING MIXTURE

The stuffing for a galantine is very quick to make as it involves no cooking. It should be made while the stock is simmering in order to save time. Weigh the boned meat to see how much stuffing you can make. You can have anything up to half the weight of the boned meat, depending on the number of people you wish to serve. Allow 175 g [6 oz] gross weight per portion.

FOR A 1.25 KG [2 LB 12 OZ]
CHICKEN,
BONED WEIGHT
225 g [½ lb] lean veal
225 g [½ lb] lean pork
75 g [3 oz] lean ham
50 g [2 oz] fresh white
   breadcrumbs
1 onion
freshly ground black pepper
15 ml [1 tablespoon] freshly
   chopped parsley

Star recipe

Chicken Kiev

◩◩◩ *The secrets of perfect chicken Kiev come in chilling the centre thoroughly beforehand, so that it melts gradually throughout the frying process; in using fresh, home-made breadcrumbs and not the ready-made ones to which busy restaurants so often resort; and in heating the oil to the exact temperature specified, in order that both the breadcrumb coating and the chicken within are fried to perfection and no more. If the oil is too hot, the outside browns while the chicken inside is still half raw; if the oil is not hot enough, it soaks right through the coating making the dish soggy.*

An infallible way of achieving the right oil temperature is by using a thermometer, unless you have an electric controlled-temperature deep frier.

For a stylish finished effect, bone chicken portions but do it in such a way that the end of the leg bone is left attached. If desired, this can be covered with a paper frill at the serving stage. For this effect, buy chicken portions made up of the leg and a piece of breast.

SERVES 6
6 chicken portions, weighing about 125-175 g [4-6 oz] each with bone
175 g [6 oz] unsalted softened butter
1 lemon
salt
freshly ground black pepper
4 garlic cloves
45 ml [3 tablespoons] freshly chopped parsley
30 ml [2 tablespoons] plain flour
freshly ground black pepper
4 medium eggs
275 g [10 oz] fresh white breadcrumbs
oil for deep frying

For the garnish:
lemon wedges
sprigs of parsley

1 Use a sharp knife to bone the chicken portions, leaving the small bone at the end of the leg attached to each of the pieces. Boning is not essential but as well as improving appearance it makes eating easier.

2 Place the butter in a bowl. Grate three-quarters of the zest off the lemon into it. Beat the butter and lemon zest together.

3 Squeeze the lemon and add the juice slowly to the butter mixture, beating all the time. Mix in the seasoning.

4 Skin and crush the garlic and add to the bowl. Add the parsley and stir well.

5 Transfer the butter mixture to a sheet of greaseproof paper. Form into a roll and chill in the refrigerator for at least 1 hour.

6 When the butter is firm, divide it into six. Take the prepared chicken portions and place a piece of the butter in the centre of each piece of chicken. Roll the chicken up round the butter and secure with a cocktail stick.

7 Season the flour and put in a polythene bag.

8 Beat the eggs and pour on to a large plate.

9 Tip the breadcrumbs into another polythene bag.

10 Lightly coat each piece of chicken by tossing in the bag of seasoned flour, then brush with beaten egg and finally toss in the breadcrumbs.

11 Repeat coating process. Chill in the refrigerator until required.

12 In a deep fat fryer, heat the oil to 180°C [350°F], or until it will brown a cube of bread in 60 seconds.

13 Place 3 of the chilled, coated chicken portions in the frying basket and lower into the oil. Fry for 15 minutes, until golden brown.

14 Take the basket out of the fat, remove cocktail sticks and transfer the chicken pieces to absorbent kitchen paper to drain, and then keep warm in a low oven while the other 3 chicken pieces are fried.

15 Arrange fried chicken pieces on a warm serving plate and garnish with lemon wedges and sprigs of parsley.

Star recipe

Avgolemono chicken with rice and lettuce

◩◩ *The name avgolemono shows that this dish includes eggs and lemon, a favourite combination in Greek and Turkish cooking. Tender chicken flesh and creamy lemon sauce are nicely offset by the nutty textured rice and an unusual lettuce garnish, producing a feast of a dish at relatively modest cost. This dish is an excellent example of just how good boiled chicken can be.*

SERVES 6
1 roasting chicken weighing about 1.8 kg [4 lb]
1 large lemon
1 large onion
1 large carrot
bouquet garni
2.5 ml [½ teaspoon] whole peppercorns
60 ml [4 tablespoons] fresh chives
30 ml [2 tablespoons] fresh parsley
75 g [3 oz] walnut pieces
1 large egg yolk
150 ml [¼ pt] thick cream
250 g [9 oz] long grain rice
30 ml [2 tablespoons] butter
30 ml [2 tablespoons] plain flour
salt and pepper
half a lettuce

1 Wipe the chicken inside and out. Grate the lemon zest, skin and slice the onion. Scrub and slice the carrot.

2 Place the chicken in a pan or flameproof casserole into which it fits snugly. Add the lemon zest, onion, carrot, bouquet garni and peppercorns and pour on enough warm water to cover the chicken thighs.

3 Place over medium heat and bring to simmering point. Immediately reduce heat to the lowest possible simmer, cover and leave to poach gently for 1½ hours or until the chicken is quite tender.

4 Meanwhile prepare the other ingredients. Chop 45 ml [3 tablespoons] chives and all the parsley and mix together with the nuts. Beat the egg yolk into a paste with the cream. Squeeze the lemon juice.

5 Strain the poaching stock, discarding vegetables and seasonings, and let the chicken rest in a low oven.

6 Reduce 575 ml [1 pt] of the chicken stock to 450 ml [¾ pt] by fast boiling.

7 Put the rice into a jug to measure volume. Using the remaining stock—plus a little water if necessary—measure out twice the volume of the rice in liquid.

8 Pour this liquid into a large pan, and add the rice and some salt. Place over a medium heat and bring to the boil, stirring once.

9 When boiling point is reached, lower the heat so that the water is just simmering and cover the pan. Cook for 15 minutes.

10 Meanwhile, make a roux with the butter and flour. Blend in the reduced stock and the lemon juice. Bring to the boil and simmer for 2 minutes, stirring all the time.

11 Drain the cooked rice, fluff it with a fork and stir in most of the nuts, chives and parsley. Arrange the rice mixture on a warm serving dish. Keep warm.

12 Joint the chicken into six pieces (see pages 6–7), skin and arrange on rice. Keep warm.

13 Blend a few tablespoons of the hot sauce into the egg and cream liaison, then carefully stir this mixture into the saucepan. Reheat very gently without boiling.

14 Season to taste with salt and pepper and pour the sauce over the chicken. Garnish with remaining herb and nut mixture, cover and keep warm.

15 Wash and shred the lettuce. Place in a colander and pour boiling water over it. Drain, salt and arrange the lettuce garnish in a ring round the dish. Chop the remaining chives over the sauce to decorate.

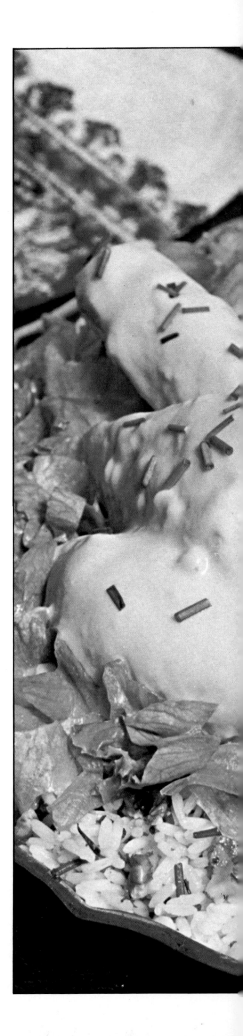

ROAST DUCK WITH ORANGE SAUCE

☒☒ *This is one of the most famous of all roast duck dishes, canard à l'orange. Unfortunately, it is also one of the most maligned. Too often the sauce is too sweet and marmaladey, ruining the flavour of the duck.*

The giblet stock which is needed for the sauce should be made in advance, as the sauce is made while the duck is roasting. Madeira or red wine may be used in place of the port.

This is one instance where the duck must be served whole and portioned at table. Serve the duck surrounded by slices of orange and add some watercress or mint for colour. Garnish the breast with unpeeled, halved orange slices and serve the sauce separately.

SERVES 2
1.4 kg [3 lb] oven-ready duck
4 thin-skinned oranges

30 ml [2 tablespoons] granulated sugar
60 ml [4 tablespoons] red wine vinegar
300 ml [½ pt] giblet stock
15 ml [1 tablespoon] arrowroot
175 ml [6 fl oz] port
1 lemon
30 ml [2 tablespoons] orange flavoured liqueur or juice
25 g [1 oz] butter

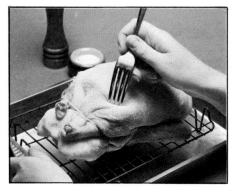

1 Heat the oven to 220°C [425°F] gas mark 7. Prepare duck for roasting and roast as described.

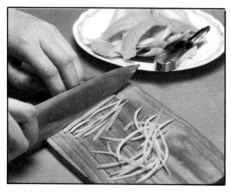

2 Meanwhile, peel 2 of the oranges with a vegetable peeler. Cut the peel into julienne strips.

3 Place strips in a pan and cover with water. Bring to boil. Simmer for 15 minutes. Drain well.

4 Put sugar and vinegar in a pan. Bring to boil. Boil rapidly for 5 minutes to caramelize.

5 Remove from heat and add 150 ml [¼ pt] stock. Stir over low heat to release caramel from pan.

6 Add remaining stock, bring to the boil, reduce heat again and simmer for 2 minutes. Squeeze lemon.

7 Blend arrowroot with 30 ml [2 tablespoons] port. Add a little of the hot sauce and blend well.

8 Stir this into the sauce. Add lemon juice and reserved peel. Simmer for 3 minutes and set aside.

9 Keep half an orange for garnish. Peel, remove pith and slice other oranges across the segments.

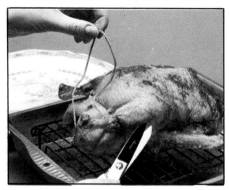

10 Remove the cooked duck from the oven. Remove trussing and leave in warm place on serving plate.

11 Tip fat from roasting tin. Add remaining port. Boil, stirring, to reduce to 45 ml [3 tablespoons].

12 Warm the sauce over low heat. Strain in port reduction and simmer. Stir in liqueur and butter.

Star recipe

CHICKEN DRUMSTICKS EN CROUTE

Encasing chicken drumsticks is one of the easiest and most attractive ways of wrapping food in pastry. Drumsticks do not take very long to cook, so they can be prepared and wrapped in the pastry well in advance. This means that drumstick parcels are the ideal choice for buffets, picnics and parties. To make them in advance, cook the meat and allow it to cool. Then you can wrap the pastry round and leave the parcels in the refrigerator until needed. Bake them immediately before eating. They do not, however, have to be served hot.

SERVES 6
6 chicken drumsticks
30 ml [2 tablespoons] vegetable oil
salt and pepper
30 ml [2 tablespoons] French mustard
225 g [½ lb] rough puff or flaky pastry
beaten egg to glaze

1 Skin and wipe drumsticks. Heat oil in a pan and add drumsticks. Fry for 5–10 minutes until browned.

2 Drain drumsticks and allow to cool. Using a small, sharp knife, slash flesh at 1.2 cm [½"] intervals.

3 Sprinkle drumsticks liberally with salt and pepper. Spread the mustard into the slashes in the flesh.

4 Heat oven to 220°C [425°F] gas mark 7. Roll pastry 3 mm [⅛"] thick to 25 × 33 cm [10 × 13"].

5 Trim edges and cut pastry into strips 2.5 cm [1"] wide, each about 30 cm [12"] long.

6 Brush edges with beaten egg. From thick end of each drumstick wind pastry strips pressing to join.

7 Continue winding the pastry strips, joining the ends if necessary, and pressing well.

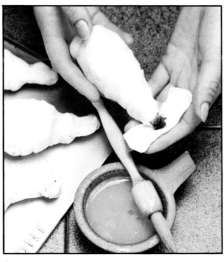

8 Finish winding the pastry at the knuckle end on each drumstick and seal with egg if necessary.

9 Use trimmings to cover knuckle ends. Place drumstick on baking sheet and relax 30 minutes.

10 Brush chicken parcels with egg and bake in centre of oven for 25 minutes. Serve immediately.

Star recipe

COQ AU VIN ROUGE

The basis of this great classic dish is a richly flavoured glossy wine sauce embracing tender portions of chicken. The traditional garnish of tiny onions, button mushrooms, little pieces of fat bacon and crisply fried bread croûtons is an important feature of the dish.

This elegant dish needs a robust full-flavoured wine, preferably from the Burgundy, Mâcon or Beaujolais areas. When a particular wine is used the dish takes the name of the wine, thus Coq au Beaujolais, or, for a really splendid occasion Coq au Chambertin.

There are many versions of the recipe. The rich flavour of this one is achieved by reducing the wine beforehand so that its concentrated essences permeate and flavour the pieces of chicken more effectively during the relatively short cooking period. It is also

flamed in brandy to further enhance the flavour, and is finally thickened with a beurre manié.

The fried bread croûtons are decorated for an addition of colour by dipping one corner first into softened butter and then into finely chopped parsley.

The short cooking period makes it more economical to use the top of the cooker although the oven could be used for the simmering if it is already in use at the correct low temperature. Considerable preparation and attention to detail are necessary to make a really good coq au vin, but the results justify its reputation.

SERVES 4
**1 roasting chicken weighing
    1.1–1.4 kg [2½–3 lb]
5 ml [1 teaspoon] tomato purée
half a chicken stock cube**

**1 small onion
salt
freshly ground black pepper
1 large garlic clove
1 bay leaf
1 sprig thyme
400 ml [¾ pt] robust red wine
100 g [¼ lb] sliced pickled
    belly pork
12 button onions
15 ml [1 tablespoon] oil
45 g [1¾ oz] butter
60 ml [4 tablespoons] brandy
175 g [6 oz] small button
    mushrooms**

For the beurre manié:
**15 ml [1 tablespoon] flour
20 g [¾ oz] softened butter**

For the garnish:
**12 triangles of white bread
freshly chopped parsley**

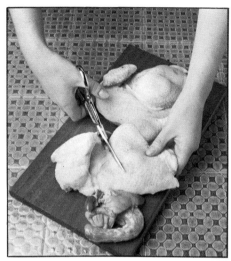

1 Wash the chicken and giblets in cold water. Drain. Quarter chicken. Cover it and refrigerate.

2 Cover chicken giblets and trimmings with water. Add the stock cube and tomato purée.

3 Peel and slice the onion and add to pan. Season and simmer for 30 minutes. Strain. Reserve liquid.

7 Heat oil and butter in frying-pan. Brown lardons and fry onions for 5 minutes. Remove and reserve.

8 Fry seasoned chicken in the pan, skin downwards, until gold. Turn and fry for 1–2 minutes.

9 Transfer chicken to flameproof casserole. Flame with warmed brandy. Add onions and lardons.

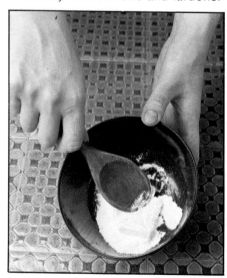

13 Remove the mushrooms, onions and lardons. Place around the chicken and keep hot.

14 There should be about 400 ml [¾ pt] sauce. Concentrate it, if necessary, by boiling, and season.

15 Skim off any surplus fat. In a bowl cream together the flour and the softened butter.

4 Meanwhile, peel and slice garlic and put in a pan with the bay leaf, thyme and red wine.

5 Simmer for about 15 minutes over a medium heat, uncovered, until the quantity is reduced by half.

6 Trim the rind from the pork and slice into lardons 6 × 25 mm [¼ × 1″]. Peel the onions.

10 Strain wine over chicken. Add the stock, cover, and simmer very gently for 40 minutes.

11 Wipe the mushroom caps and trim the stalks. Add to the casserole and simmer for 5 minutes.

12 With a slotted spoon remove the chicken and arrange in a warmed shallow serving dish.

16 Whisk this into the sauce over a low heat, piece by piece. Simmer the sauce for a few minutes.

17 While the sauce is simmering fry the bread triangles in very hot fat over medium heat.

18 Pour the thickened, glossy sauce over the chicken and garnish with oroûtons and parsley.